C-3010 CAREER EXAMINATION SERIES

This is your
PASSBOOK for...

Supervisor of Housing Caretakers

Test Preparation Study Guide
Questions & Answers

COPYRIGHT NOTICE

This book is SOLELY intended for, is sold ONLY to, and its use is RESTRICTED to individual, bona fide applicants or candidates who qualify by virtue of having seriously filed applications for appropriate license, certificate, professional and/or promotional advancement, higher school matriculation, scholarship, or other legitimate requirements of education and/or governmental authorities.

This book is NOT intended for use, class instruction, tutoring, training, duplication, copying, reprinting, excerption, or adaptation, etc., by:

1) Other publishers
2) Proprietors and/or Instructors of "Coaching" and/or Preparatory Courses
3) Personnel and/or Training Divisions of commercial, industrial, and governmental organizations
4) Schools, colleges, or universities and/or their departments and staffs, including teachers and other personnel
5) Testing Agencies or Bureaus
6) Study groups which seek by the purchase of a single volume to copy and/or duplicate and/or adapt this material for use by the group as a whole without having purchased individual volumes for each of the members of the group
7) Et al.

Such persons would be in violation of appropriate Federal and State statutes.

PROVISION OF LICENSING AGREEMENTS – Recognized educational, commercial, industrial, and governmental institutions and organizations, and others legitimately engaged in educational pursuits, including training, testing, and measurement activities, may address request for a licensing agreement to the copyright owners, who will determine whether, and under what conditions, including fees and charges, the materials in this book may be used them. In other words, a licensing facility exists for the legitimate use of the material in this book on other than an individual basis. However, it is asseverated and affirmed here that the material in this book CANNOT be used without the receipt of the express permission of such a licensing agreement from the Publishers. Inquiries re licensing should be addressed to the company, attention rights and permissions department.

All rights reserved, including the right of reproduction in whole or in part, in any form or by any means, electronic or mechanical, including photocopying, recording, or by any information storage and retrieval system, without permission in writing from the Publisher.

Copyright © 2024 by
National Learning Corporation

212 Michael Drive, Syosset, NY 11791
(516) 921-8888 • www.passbooks.com
E-mail: info@passbooks.com

PUBLISHED IN THE UNITED STATES OF AMERICA

PASSBOOK® SERIES

THE *PASSBOOK® SERIES* has been created to prepare applicants and candidates for the ultimate academic battlefield – the examination room.

At some time in our lives, each and every one of us may be required to take an examination – for validation, matriculation, admission, qualification, registration, certification, or licensure.

Based on the assumption that every applicant or candidate has met the basic formal educational standards, has taken the required number of courses, and read the necessary texts, the *PASSBOOK® SERIES* furnishes the one special preparation which may assure passing with confidence, instead of failing with insecurity. Examination questions – together with answers – are furnished as the basic vehicle for study so that the mysteries of the examination and its compounding difficulties may be eliminated or diminished by a sure method.

This book is meant to help you pass your examination provided that you qualify and are serious in your objective.

The entire field is reviewed through the huge store of content information which is succinctly presented through a provocative and challenging approach – the question-and-answer method.

A climate of success is established by furnishing the correct answers at the end of each test.

You soon learn to recognize types of questions, forms of questions, and patterns of questioning. You may even begin to anticipate expected outcomes.

You perceive that many questions are repeated or adapted so that you can gain acute insights, which may enable you to score many sure points.

You learn how to confront new questions, or types of questions, and to attack them confidently and work out the correct answers.

You note objectives and emphases, and recognize pitfalls and dangers, so that you may make positive educational adjustments.

Moreover, you are kept fully informed in relation to new concepts, methods, practices, and directions in the field.

You discover that you are actually taking the examination all the time: you are preparing for the examination by "taking" an examination, not by reading extraneous and/or supererogatory textbooks.

In short, this PASSBOOK®, used directedly, should be an important factor in helping you to pass your test.

SUPERVISOR OF HOUSING CARETAKERS

DUTIES AND RESPONSIBILITIES
Under supervision, instructs and supervises the Housing Caretakers responsible for cleaning and maintaining the grounds, public spaces, and stair halls of public housing projects in proper condition; performs related work.

EXAMPLES OF TYPICAL TASKS
Makes assignments, trains, and checks performance of Housing Caretakers; reports move-ins and move-outs; handles tenant lockouts; fills out work orders as a result of apartment inspections; assists in inspection of buildings and equipment; operates or directs the operation of mechanical-electrical equipment such as outdoor vacuum cleaners, snow plows, etc.; reports any hazardous conditions observed in any part of the project.

SCOPE OF THE EXAMINATION
The multiple-choice written test may include questions on supervision of subordinates as related to janitorial work; proper cleaning procedures, safety, security, and training; inspection and evaluation of housing project buildings and grounds and determination of work requirements; preparation and review of inspection forms, reports, work orders, and log entries; tools and equipment; clerical abilities; arithmetic; reading comprehension; writing and other related items.

HOW TO TAKE A TEST

I. YOU MUST PASS AN EXAMINATION

A. WHAT EVERY CANDIDATE SHOULD KNOW

Examination applicants often ask us for help in preparing for the written test. What can I study in advance? What kinds of questions will be asked? How will the test be given? How will the papers be graded?

As an applicant for a civil service examination, you may be wondering about some of these things. Our purpose here is to suggest effective methods of advance study and to describe civil service examinations.

Your chances for success on this examination can be increased if you know how to prepare. Those "pre-examination jitters" can be reduced if you know what to expect. You can even experience an adventure in good citizenship if you know why civil service exams are given.

B. WHY ARE CIVIL SERVICE EXAMINATIONS GIVEN?

Civil service examinations are important to you in two ways. As a citizen, you want public jobs filled by employees who know how to do their work. As a job seeker, you want a fair chance to compete for that job on an equal footing with other candidates. The best-known means of accomplishing this two-fold goal is the competitive examination.

Exams are widely publicized throughout the nation. They may be administered for jobs in federal, state, city, municipal, town or village governments or agencies.

Any citizen may apply, with some limitations, such as the age or residence of applicants. Your experience and education may be reviewed to see whether you meet the requirements for the particular examination. When these requirements exist, they are reasonable and applied consistently to all applicants. Thus, a competitive examination may cause you some uneasiness now, but it is your privilege and safeguard.

C. HOW ARE CIVIL SERVICE EXAMS DEVELOPED?

Examinations are carefully written by trained technicians who are specialists in the field known as "psychological measurement," in consultation with recognized authorities in the field of work that the test will cover. These experts recommend the subject matter areas or skills to be tested; only those knowledges or skills important to your success on the job are included. The most reliable books and source materials available are used as references. Together, the experts and technicians judge the difficulty level of the questions.

Test technicians know how to phrase questions so that the problem is clearly stated. Their ethics do not permit "trick" or "catch" questions. Questions may have been tried out on sample groups, or subjected to statistical analysis, to determine their usefulness.

Written tests are often used in combination with performance tests, ratings of training and experience, and oral interviews. All of these measures combine to form the best-known means of finding the right person for the right job.

II. HOW TO PASS THE WRITTEN TEST

A. NATURE OF THE EXAMINATION

To prepare intelligently for civil service examinations, you should know how they differ from school examinations you have taken. In school you were assigned certain definite pages to read or subjects to cover. The examination questions were quite detailed and usually emphasized memory. Civil service exams, on the other hand, try to discover your present ability to perform the duties of a position, plus your potentiality to learn these duties. In other words, a civil service exam attempts to predict how successful you will be. Questions cover such a broad area that they cannot be as minute and detailed as school exam questions.

In the public service similar kinds of work, or positions, are grouped together in one "class." This process is known as *position-classification*. All the positions in a class are paid according to the salary range for that class. One class title covers all of these positions, and they are all tested by the same examination.

B. FOUR BASIC STEPS

1) Study the announcement

How, then, can you know what subjects to study? Our best answer is: "Learn as much as possible about the class of positions for which you've applied." The exam will test the knowledge, skills and abilities needed to do the work.

Your most valuable source of information about the position you want is the official exam announcement. This announcement lists the training and experience qualifications. Check these standards and apply only if you come reasonably close to meeting them.

The brief description of the position in the examination announcement offers some clues to the subjects which will be tested. Think about the job itself. Review the duties in your mind. Can you perform them, or are there some in which you are rusty? Fill in the blank spots in your preparation.

Many jurisdictions preview the written test in the exam announcement by including a section called "Knowledge and Abilities Required," "Scope of the Examination," or some similar heading. Here you will find out specifically what fields will be tested.

2) Review your own background

Once you learn in general what the position is all about, and what you need to know to do the work, ask yourself which subjects you already know fairly well and which need improvement. You may wonder whether to concentrate on improving your strong areas or on building some background in your fields of weakness. When the announcement has specified "some knowledge" or "considerable knowledge," or has used adjectives like "beginning principles of..." or "advanced ... methods," you can get a clue as to the number and difficulty of questions to be asked in any given field. More questions, and hence broader coverage, would be included for those subjects which are more important in the work. Now weigh your strengths and weaknesses against the job requirements and prepare accordingly.

3) Determine the level of the position

Another way to tell how intensively you should prepare is to understand the level of the job for which you are applying. Is it the entering level? In other words, is this the position in which beginners in a field of work are hired? Or is it an intermediate or advanced level? Sometimes this is indicated by such words as "Junior" or "Senior" in the class title. Other jurisdictions use Roman numerals to designate the level – Clerk I, Clerk II, for example. The word "Supervisor" sometimes appears in the title. If the level is not indicated by the title, check the description of duties. Will you be working under very close supervision, or will you have responsibility for independent decisions in this work?

4) Choose appropriate study materials

Now that you know the subjects to be examined and the relative amount of each subject to be covered, you can choose suitable study materials. For beginning level jobs, or even advanced ones, if you have a pronounced weakness in some aspect of your training, read a modern, standard textbook in that field. Be sure it is up to date and has general coverage. Such books are normally available at your library, and the librarian will be glad to help you locate one. For entry-level positions, questions of appropriate difficulty are chosen – neither highly advanced questions, nor those too simple. Such questions require careful thought but not advanced training.

If the position for which you are applying is technical or advanced, you will read more advanced, specialized material. If you are already familiar with the basic principles of your field, elementary textbooks would waste your time. Concentrate on advanced textbooks and technical periodicals. Think through the concepts and review difficult problems in your field.

These are all general sources. You can get more ideas on your own initiative, following these leads. For example, training manuals and publications of the government agency which employs workers in your field can be useful, particularly for technical and professional positions. A letter or visit to the government department involved may result in more specific study suggestions, and certainly will provide you with a more definite idea of the exact nature of the position you are seeking.

III. KINDS OF TESTS

Tests are used for purposes other than measuring knowledge and ability to perform specified duties. For some positions, it is equally important to test ability to make adjustments to new situations or to profit from training. In others, basic mental abilities not dependent on information are essential. Questions which test these things may not appear as pertinent to the duties of the position as those which test for knowledge and information. Yet they are often highly important parts of a fair examination. For very general questions, it is almost impossible to help you direct your study efforts. What we can do is to point out some of the more common of these general abilities needed in public service positions and describe some typical questions.

1) General information

Broad, general information has been found useful for predicting job success in some kinds of work. This is tested in a variety of ways, from vocabulary lists to questions about current events. Basic background in some field of work, such as sociology or economics, may be sampled in a group of questions. Often these are principles which have become familiar to most persons through exposure rather than through formal training. It is difficult to advise you how to study for these questions; being alert to the world around you is our best suggestion.

2) Verbal ability

An example of an ability needed in many positions is verbal or language ability. Verbal ability is, in brief, the ability to use and understand words. Vocabulary and grammar tests are typical measures of this ability. Reading comprehension or paragraph interpretation questions are common in many kinds of civil service tests. You are given a paragraph of written material and asked to find its central meaning.

3) Numerical ability

Number skills can be tested by the familiar arithmetic problem, by checking paired lists of numbers to see which are alike and which are different, or by interpreting charts and graphs. In the latter test, a graph may be printed in the test booklet which you are asked to use as the basis for answering questions.

4) Observation

A popular test for law-enforcement positions is the observation test. A picture is shown to you for several minutes, then taken away. Questions about the picture test your ability to observe both details and larger elements.

5) Following directions

In many positions in the public service, the employee must be able to carry out written instructions dependably and accurately. You may be given a chart with several columns, each column listing a variety of information. The questions require you to carry out directions involving the information given in the chart.

6) Skills and aptitudes

Performance tests effectively measure some manual skills and aptitudes. When the skill is one in which you are trained, such as typing or shorthand, you can practice. These tests are often very much like those given in business school or high school courses. For many of the other skills and aptitudes, however, no short-time preparation can be made. Skills and abilities natural to you or that you have developed throughout your lifetime are being tested.

Many of the general questions just described provide all the data needed to answer the questions and ask you to use your reasoning ability to find the answers. Your best preparation for these tests, as well as for tests of facts and ideas, is to be at your physical and mental best. You, no doubt, have your own methods of getting into an exam-taking mood and keeping "in shape." The next section lists some ideas on this subject.

IV. KINDS OF QUESTIONS

Only rarely is the "essay" question, which you answer in narrative form, used in civil service tests. Civil service tests are usually of the short-answer type. Full instructions for answering these questions will be given to you at the examination. But in case this is your first experience with short-answer questions and separate answer sheets, here is what you need to know:

1) **Multiple-choice Questions**

Most popular of the short-answer questions is the "multiple choice" or "best answer" question. It can be used, for example, to test for factual knowledge, ability to solve problems or judgment in meeting situations found at work.

A multiple-choice question is normally one of three types—
- It can begin with an incomplete statement followed by several possible endings. You are to find the one ending which *best* completes the statement, although some of the others may not be entirely wrong.
- It can also be a complete statement in the form of a question which is answered by choosing one of the statements listed.

- It can be in the form of a problem – again you select the best answer.

Here is an example of a multiple-choice question with a discussion which should give you some clues as to the method for choosing the right answer:

When an employee has a complaint about his assignment, the action which will *best* help him overcome his difficulty is to
  A. discuss his difficulty with his coworkers
  B. take the problem to the head of the organization
  C. take the problem to the person who gave him the assignment
  D. say nothing to anyone about his complaint

In answering this question, you should study each of the choices to find which is best. Consider choice "A" – Certainly an employee may discuss his complaint with fellow employees, but no change or improvement can result, and the complaint remains unresolved. Choice "B" is a poor choice since the head of the organization probably does not know what assignment you have been given, and taking your problem to him is known as "going over the head" of the supervisor. The supervisor, or person who made the assignment, is the person who can clarify it or correct any injustice. Choice "C" is, therefore, correct. To say nothing, as in choice "D," is unwise. Supervisors have and interest in knowing the problems employees are facing, and the employee is seeking a solution to his problem.

2) True/False Questions

The "true/false" or "right/wrong" form of question is sometimes used. Here a complete statement is given. Your job is to decide whether the statement is right or wrong.

SAMPLE: A roaming cell-phone call to a nearby city costs less than a non-roaming call to a distant city.

This statement is wrong, or false, since roaming calls are more expensive.

This is not a complete list of all possible question forms, although most of the others are variations of these common types. You will always get complete directions for answering questions. Be sure you understand *how* to mark your answers – ask questions until you do.

V. RECORDING YOUR ANSWERS

Computer terminals are used more and more today for many different kinds of exams.
For an examination with very few applicants, you may be told to record your answers in the test booklet itself. Separate answer sheets are much more common. If this separate answer sheet is to be scored by machine – and this is often the case – it is highly important that you mark your answers correctly in order to get credit.
An electronic scoring machine is often used in civil service offices because of the speed with which papers can be scored. Machine-scored answer sheets must be marked with a pencil, which will be given to you. This pencil has a high graphite content which responds to the electronic scoring machine. As a matter of fact, stray dots may register as answers, so do not let your pencil rest on the answer sheet while you are pondering the correct answer. Also, if your pencil lead breaks or is otherwise defective, ask for another.

Since the answer sheet will be dropped in a slot in the scoring machine, be careful not to bend the corners or get the paper crumpled.

The answer sheet normally has five vertical columns of numbers, with 30 numbers to a column. These numbers correspond to the question numbers in your test booklet. After each number, going across the page are four or five pairs of dotted lines. These short dotted lines have small letters or numbers above them. The first two pairs may also have a "T" or "F" above the letters. This indicates that the first two pairs only are to be used if the questions are of the true-false type. If the questions are multiple choice, disregard the "T" and "F" and pay attention only to the small letters or numbers.

Answer your questions in the manner of the sample that follows:

32. The largest city in the United States is
    A. Washington, D.C.
    B. New York City
    C. Chicago
    D. Detroit
    E. San Francisco

1) Choose the answer you think is best. (New York City is the largest, so "B" is correct.)
2) Find the row of dotted lines numbered the same as the question you are answering. (Find row number 32)
3) Find the pair of dotted lines corresponding to the answer. (Find the pair of lines under the mark "B.")
4) Make a solid black mark between the dotted lines.

VI. BEFORE THE TEST

Common sense will help you find procedures to follow to get ready for an examination. Too many of us, however, overlook these sensible measures. Indeed, nervousness and fatigue have been found to be the most serious reasons why applicants fail to do their best on civil service tests. Here is a list of reminders:

- Begin your preparation early – Don't wait until the last minute to go scurrying around for books and materials or to find out what the position is all about.
- Prepare continuously – An hour a night for a week is better than an all-night cram session. This has been definitely established. What is more, a night a week for a month will return better dividends than crowding your study into a shorter period of time.
- Locate the place of the exam – You have been sent a notice telling you when and where to report for the examination. If the location is in a different town or otherwise unfamiliar to you, it would be well to inquire the best route and learn something about the building.
- Relax the night before the test – Allow your mind to rest. Do not study at all that night. Plan some mild recreation or diversion; then go to bed early and get a good night's sleep.
- Get up early enough to make a leisurely trip to the place for the test – This way unforeseen events, traffic snarls, unfamiliar buildings, etc. will not upset you.
- Dress comfortably – A written test is not a fashion show. You will be known by number and not by name, so wear something comfortable.

- Leave excess paraphernalia at home – Shopping bags and odd bundles will get in your way. You need bring only the items mentioned in the official notice you received; usually everything you need is provided. Do not bring reference books to the exam. They will only confuse those last minutes and be taken away from you when in the test room.
- Arrive somewhat ahead of time – If because of transportation schedules you must get there very early, bring a newspaper or magazine to take your mind off yourself while waiting.
- Locate the examination room – When you have found the proper room, you will be directed to the seat or part of the room where you will sit. Sometimes you are given a sheet of instructions to read while you are waiting. Do not fill out any forms until you are told to do so; just read them and be prepared.
- Relax and prepare to listen to the instructions
- If you have any physical problem that may keep you from doing your best, be sure to tell the test administrator. If you are sick or in poor health, you really cannot do your best on the exam. You can come back and take the test some other time.

VII. AT THE TEST

The day of the test is here and you have the test booklet in your hand. The temptation to get going is very strong. Caution! There is more to success than knowing the right answers. You must know how to identify your papers and understand variations in the type of short-answer question used in this particular examination. Follow these suggestions for maximum results from your efforts:

1) Cooperate with the monitor

The test administrator has a duty to create a situation in which you can be as much at ease as possible. He will give instructions, tell you when to begin, check to see that you are marking your answer sheet correctly, and so on. He is not there to guard you, although he will see that your competitors do not take unfair advantage. He wants to help you do your best.

2) Listen to all instructions

Don't jump the gun! Wait until you understand all directions. In most civil service tests you get more time than you need to answer the questions. So don't be in a hurry. Read each word of instructions until you clearly understand the meaning. Study the examples, listen to all announcements and follow directions. Ask questions if you do not understand what to do.

3) Identify your papers

Civil service exams are usually identified by number only. You will be assigned a number; you must not put your name on your test papers. Be sure to copy your number correctly. Since more than one exam may be given, copy your exact examination title.

4) Plan your time

Unless you are told that a test is a "speed" or "rate of work" test, speed itself is usually not important. Time enough to answer all the questions will be provided, but this does not mean that you have all day. An overall time limit has been set. Divide the total time (in minutes) by the number of questions to determine the approximate time you have for each question.

5) Do not linger over difficult questions

If you come across a difficult question, mark it with a paper clip (useful to have along) and come back to it when you have been through the booklet. One caution if you do this – be sure to skip a number on your answer sheet as well. Check often to be sure that you have not lost your place and that you are marking in the row numbered the same as the question you are answering.

6) Read the questions

Be sure you know what the question asks! Many capable people are unsuccessful because they failed to *read* the questions correctly.

7) Answer all questions

Unless you have been instructed that a penalty will be deducted for incorrect answers, it is better to guess than to omit a question.

8) Speed tests

It is often better NOT to guess on speed tests. It has been found that on timed tests people are tempted to spend the last few seconds before time is called in marking answers at random – without even reading them – in the hope of picking up a few extra points. To discourage this practice, the instructions may warn you that your score will be "corrected" for guessing. That is, a penalty will be applied. The incorrect answers will be deducted from the correct ones, or some other penalty formula will be used.

9) Review your answers

If you finish before time is called, go back to the questions you guessed or omitted to give them further thought. Review other answers if you have time.

10) Return your test materials

If you are ready to leave before others have finished or time is called, take ALL your materials to the monitor and leave quietly. Never take any test material with you. The monitor can discover whose papers are not complete, and taking a test booklet may be grounds for disqualification.

VIII. EXAMINATION TECHNIQUES

1) Read the general instructions carefully. These are usually printed on the first page of the exam booklet. As a rule, these instructions refer to the timing of the examination; the fact that you should not start work until the signal and must stop work at a signal, etc. If there are any *special* instructions, such as a choice of questions to be answered, make sure that you note this instruction carefully.

2) When you are ready to start work on the examination, that is as soon as the signal has been given, read the instructions to each question booklet, underline any key words or phrases, such as *least, best, outline, describe* and the like. In this way you will tend to answer as requested rather than discover on reviewing your paper that you *listed without describing*, that you selected the *worst* choice rather than the *best* choice, etc.

3) If the examination is of the objective or multiple-choice type – that is, each question will also give a series of possible answers: A, B, C or D, and you are called upon to select the best answer and write the letter next to that answer on your answer paper – it is advisable to start answering each question in turn. There may be anywhere from 50 to 100 such questions in the three or four hours allotted and you can see how much time would be taken if you read through all the questions before beginning to answer any. Furthermore, if you come across a question or group of questions which you know would be difficult to answer, it would undoubtedly affect your handling of all the other questions.

4) If the examination is of the essay type and contains but a few questions, it is a moot point as to whether you should read all the questions before starting to answer any one. Of course, if you are given a choice – say five out of seven and the like – then it is essential to read all the questions so you can eliminate the two that are most difficult. If, however, you are asked to answer all the questions, there may be danger in trying to answer the easiest one first because you may find that you will spend too much time on it. The best technique is to answer the first question, then proceed to the second, etc.

5) Time your answers. Before the exam begins, write down the time it started, then add the time allowed for the examination and write down the time it must be completed, then divide the time available somewhat as follows:
   - If 3-1/2 hours are allowed, that would be 210 minutes. If you have 80 objective-type questions, that would be an average of 2-1/2 minutes per question. Allow yourself no more than 2 minutes per question, or a total of 160 minutes, which will permit about 50 minutes to review.
   - If for the time allotment of 210 minutes there are 7 essay questions to answer, that would average about 30 minutes a question. Give yourself only 25 minutes per question so that you have about 35 minutes to review.

6) The most important instruction is to *read each question* and make sure you know what is wanted. The second most important instruction is to *time yourself properly* so that you answer every question. The third most important instruction is to *answer every question*. Guess if you have to but include something for each question. Remember that you will receive no credit for a blank and will probably receive some credit if you write something in answer to an essay question. If you guess a letter – say "B" for a multiple-choice question – you may have guessed right. If you leave a blank as an answer to a multiple-choice question, the examiners may respect your feelings but it will not add a point to your score. Some exams may penalize you for wrong answers, so in such cases *only*, you may not want to guess unless you have some basis for your answer.

7) Suggestions
   a. Objective-type questions
      1. Examine the question booklet for proper sequence of pages and questions
      2. Read all instructions carefully
      3. Skip any question which seems too difficult; return to it after all other questions have been answered
      4. Apportion your time properly; do not spend too much time on any single question or group of questions

5. Note and underline key words – *all, most, fewest, least, best, worst, same, opposite,* etc.
6. Pay particular attention to negatives
7. Note unusual option, e.g., unduly long, short, complex, different or similar in content to the body of the question
8. Observe the use of "hedging" words – *probably, may, most likely,* etc.
9. Make sure that your answer is put next to the same number as the question
10. Do not second-guess unless you have good reason to believe the second answer is definitely more correct
11. Cross out original answer if you decide another answer is more accurate; do not erase until you are ready to hand your paper in
12. Answer all questions; guess unless instructed otherwise
13. Leave time for review

   b. Essay questions
1. Read each question carefully
2. Determine exactly what is wanted. Underline key words or phrases.
3. Decide on outline or paragraph answer
4. Include many different points and elements unless asked to develop any one or two points or elements
5. Show impartiality by giving pros and cons unless directed to select one side only
6. Make and write down any assumptions you find necessary to answer the questions
7. Watch your English, grammar, punctuation and choice of words
8. Time your answers; don't crowd material

8) Answering the essay question

Most essay questions can be answered by framing the specific response around several key words or ideas. Here are a few such key words or ideas:

M's: manpower, materials, methods, money, management
P's: purpose, program, policy, plan, procedure, practice, problems, pitfalls, personnel, public relations

   a. Six basic steps in handling problems:
1. Preliminary plan and background development
2. Collect information, data and facts
3. Analyze and interpret information, data and facts
4. Analyze and develop solutions as well as make recommendations
5. Prepare report and sell recommendations
6. Install recommendations and follow up effectiveness

   b. Pitfalls to avoid
1. *Taking things for granted* – A statement of the situation does not necessarily imply that each of the elements is necessarily true; for example, a complaint may be invalid and biased so that all that can be taken for granted is that a complaint has been registered

2. *Considering only one side of a situation* – Wherever possible, indicate several alternatives and then point out the reasons you selected the best one
3. *Failing to indicate follow up* – Whenever your answer indicates action on your part, make certain that you will take proper follow-up action to see how successful your recommendations, procedures or actions turn out to be
4. *Taking too long in answering any single question* – Remember to time your answers properly

IX. AFTER THE TEST

Scoring procedures differ in detail among civil service jurisdictions although the general principles are the same. Whether the papers are hand-scored or graded by machine we have described, they are nearly always graded by number. That is, the person who marks the paper knows only the number – never the name – of the applicant. Not until all the papers have been graded will they be matched with names. If other tests, such as training and experience or oral interview ratings have been given, scores will be combined. Different parts of the examination usually have different weights. For example, the written test might count 60 percent of the final grade, and a rating of training and experience 40 percent. In many jurisdictions, veterans will have a certain number of points added to their grades.

After the final grade has been determined, the names are placed in grade order and an eligible list is established. There are various methods for resolving ties between those who get the same final grade – probably the most common is to place first the name of the person whose application was received first. Job offers are made from the eligible list in the order the names appear on it. You will be notified of your grade and your rank as soon as all these computations have been made. This will be done as rapidly as possible.

People who are found to meet the requirements in the announcement are called "eligibles." Their names are put on a list of eligible candidates. An eligible's chances of getting a job depend on how high he stands on this list and how fast agencies are filling jobs from the list.

When a job is to be filled from a list of eligibles, the agency asks for the names of people on the list of eligibles for that job. When the civil service commission receives this request, it sends to the agency the names of the three people highest on this list. Or, if the job to be filled has specialized requirements, the office sends the agency the names of the top three persons who meet these requirements from the general list.

The appointing officer makes a choice from among the three people whose names were sent to him. If the selected person accepts the appointment, the names of the others are put back on the list to be considered for future openings.

That is the rule in hiring from all kinds of eligible lists, whether they are for typist, carpenter, chemist, or something else. For every vacancy, the appointing officer has his choice of any one of the top three eligibles on the list. This explains why the person whose name is on top of the list sometimes does not get an appointment when some of the persons lower on the list do. If the appointing officer chooses the second or third eligible, the No. 1 eligible does not get a job at once, but stays on the list until he is appointed or the list is terminated.

X. HOW TO PASS THE INTERVIEW TEST

The examination for which you applied requires an oral interview test. You have already taken the written test and you are now being called for the interview test – the final part of the formal examination.

You may think that it is not possible to prepare for an interview test and that there are no procedures to follow during an interview. Our purpose is to point out some things you can do in advance that will help you and some good rules to follow and pitfalls to avoid while you are being interviewed.

What is an interview supposed to test?

The written examination is designed to test the technical knowledge and competence of the candidate; the oral is designed to evaluate intangible qualities, not readily measured otherwise, and to establish a list showing the relative fitness of each candidate – as measured against his competitors – for the position sought. Scoring is not on the basis of "right" and "wrong," but on a sliding scale of values ranging from "not passable" to "outstanding." As a matter of fact, it is possible to achieve a relatively low score without a single "incorrect" answer because of evident weakness in the qualities being measured.

Occasionally, an examination may consist entirely of an oral test – either an individual or a group oral. In such cases, information is sought concerning the technical knowledges and abilities of the candidate, since there has been no written examination for this purpose. More commonly, however, an oral test is used to supplement a written examination.

Who conducts interviews?

The composition of oral boards varies among different jurisdictions. In nearly all, a representative of the personnel department serves as chairman. One of the members of the board may be a representative of the department in which the candidate would work. In some cases, "outside experts" are used, and, frequently, a businessman or some other representative of the general public is asked to serve. Labor and management or other special groups may be represented. The aim is to secure the services of experts in the appropriate field.

However the board is composed, it is a good idea (and not at all improper or unethical) to ascertain in advance of the interview who the members are and what groups they represent. When you are introduced to them, you will have some idea of their backgrounds and interests, and at least you will not stutter and stammer over their names.

What should be done before the interview?

While knowledge about the board members is useful and takes some of the surprise element out of the interview, there is other preparation which is more substantive. It *is* possible to prepare for an oral interview – in several ways:

1) Keep a copy of your application and review it carefully before the interview

This may be the only document before the oral board, and the starting point of the interview. Know what education and experience you have listed there, and the sequence and dates of all of it. Sometimes the board will ask you to review the highlights of your experience for them; you should not have to hem and haw doing it.

2) Study the class specification and the examination announcement

Usually, the oral board has one or both of these to guide them. The qualities, characteristics or knowledges required by the position sought are stated in these documents. They offer valuable clues as to the nature of the oral interview. For example, if the job involves supervisory responsibilities, the announcement will usually indicate that knowledge of modern supervisory methods and the qualifications of the candidate as a supervisor will be tested. If so, you can expect such questions, frequently in the form of a hypothetical situation which you are expected to solve. NEVER go into an oral without knowledge of the duties and responsibilities of the job you seek.

3) Think through each qualification required

Try to visualize the kind of questions you would ask if you were a board member. How well could you answer them? Try especially to appraise your own knowledge and background in each area, *measured against the job sought*, and identify any areas in which you are weak. Be critical and realistic – do not flatter yourself.

4) Do some general reading in areas in which you feel you may be weak

For example, if the job involves supervision and your past experience has NOT, some general reading in supervisory methods and practices, particularly in the field of human relations, might be useful. Do NOT study agency procedures or detailed manuals. The oral board will be testing your understanding and capacity, not your memory.

5) Get a good night's sleep and watch your general health and mental attitude

You will want a clear head at the interview. Take care of a cold or any other minor ailment, and of course, no hangovers.

What should be done on the day of the interview?

Now comes the day of the interview itself. Give yourself plenty of time to get there. Plan to arrive somewhat ahead of the scheduled time, particularly if your appointment is in the fore part of the day. If a previous candidate fails to appear, the board might be ready for you a bit early. By early afternoon an oral board is almost invariably behind schedule if there are many candidates, and you may have to wait. Take along a book or magazine to read, or your application to review, but leave any extraneous material in the waiting room when you go in for your interview. In any event, relax and compose yourself.

The matter of dress is important. The board is forming impressions about you – from your experience, your manners, your attitude, and your appearance. Give your personal appearance careful attention. Dress your best, but not your flashiest. Choose conservative, appropriate clothing, and be sure it is immaculate. This is a business interview, and your appearance should indicate that you regard it as such. Besides, being well groomed and properly dressed will help boost your confidence.

Sooner or later, someone will call your name and escort you into the interview room. *This is it.* From here on you are on your own. It is too late for any more preparation. But remember, you asked for this opportunity to prove your fitness, and you are here because your request was granted.

What happens when you go in?

The usual sequence of events will be as follows: The clerk (who is often the board stenographer) will introduce you to the chairman of the oral board, who will introduce you to the other members of the board. Acknowledge the introductions before you sit down. Do not be surprised if you find a microphone facing you or a stenotypist sitting by. Oral interviews are usually recorded in the event of an appeal or other review.

Usually the chairman of the board will open the interview by reviewing the highlights of your education and work experience from your application – primarily for the benefit of the other members of the board, as well as to get the material into the record. Do not interrupt or comment unless there is an error or significant misinterpretation; if that is the case, do not hesitate. But do not quibble about insignificant matters. Also, he will usually ask you some question about your education, experience or your present job – partly to get you to start talking and to establish the interviewing "rapport." He may start the actual questioning, or turn it over to one of the other members. Frequently, each member undertakes the questioning on a particular area, one in which he is perhaps most competent, so you can expect each member to participate in the examination. Because time is limited, you may also expect some rather abrupt switches in the direction the questioning takes, so do not be upset by it. Normally, a board member will not pursue a single line of questioning unless he discovers a particular strength or weakness.

After each member has participated, the chairman will usually ask whether any member has any further questions, then will ask you if you have anything you wish to add. Unless you are expecting this question, it may floor you. Worse, it may start you off on an extended, extemporaneous speech. The board is not usually seeking more information. The question is principally to offer you a last opportunity to present further qualifications or to indicate that you have nothing to add. So, if you feel that a significant qualification or characteristic has been overlooked, it is proper to point it out in a sentence or so. Do not compliment the board on the thoroughness of their examination – they have been sketchy, and you know it. If you wish, merely say, "No thank you, I have nothing further to add." This is a point where you can "talk yourself out" of a good impression or fail to present an important bit of information. Remember, *you close the interview yourself.*

The chairman will then say, "That is all, Mr. _____, thank you." Do not be startled; the interview is over, and quicker than you think. Thank him, gather your belongings and take your leave. Save your sigh of relief for the other side of the door.

How to put your best foot forward

Throughout this entire process, you may feel that the board individually and collectively is trying to pierce your defenses, seek out your hidden weaknesses and embarrass and confuse you. Actually, this is not true. They are obliged to make an appraisal of your qualifications for the job you are seeking, and they want to see you in your best light. Remember, they must interview all candidates and a non-cooperative candidate may become a failure in spite of their best efforts to bring out his qualifications. Here are 15 suggestions that will help you:

1) Be natural – Keep your attitude confident, not cocky

If you are not confident that you can do the job, do not expect the board to be. Do not apologize for your weaknesses, try to bring out your strong points. The board is interested in a positive, not negative, presentation. Cockiness will antagonize any board member and make him wonder if you are covering up a weakness by a false show of strength.

2) Get comfortable, but don't lounge or sprawl

Sit erectly but not stiffly. A careless posture may lead the board to conclude that you are careless in other things, or at least that you are not impressed by the importance of the occasion. Either conclusion is natural, even if incorrect. Do not fuss with your clothing, a pencil or an ashtray. Your hands may occasionally be useful to emphasize a point; do not let them become a point of distraction.

3) Do not wisecrack or make small talk

This is a serious situation, and your attitude should show that you consider it as such. Further, the time of the board is limited – they do not want to waste it, and neither should you.

4) Do not exaggerate your experience or abilities

In the first place, from information in the application or other interviews and sources, the board may know more about you than you think. Secondly, you probably will not get away with it. An experienced board is rather adept at spotting such a situation, so do not take the chance.

5) If you know a board member, do not make a point of it, yet do not hide it

Certainly you are not fooling him, and probably not the other members of the board. Do not try to take advantage of your acquaintanceship – it will probably do you little good.

6) Do not dominate the interview

Let the board do that. They will give you the clues – do not assume that you have to do all the talking. Realize that the board has a number of questions to ask you, and do not try to take up all the interview time by showing off your extensive knowledge of the answer to the first one.

7) Be attentive

You only have 20 minutes or so, and you should keep your attention at its sharpest throughout. When a member is addressing a problem or question to you, give him your undivided attention. Address your reply principally to him, but do not exclude the other board members.

8) Do not interrupt

A board member may be stating a problem for you to analyze. He will ask you a question when the time comes. Let him state the problem, and wait for the question.

9) Make sure you understand the question

Do not try to answer until you are sure what the question is. If it is not clear, restate it in your own words or ask the board member to clarify it for you. However, do not haggle about minor elements.

10) Reply promptly but not hastily

A common entry on oral board rating sheets is "candidate responded readily," or "candidate hesitated in replies." Respond as promptly and quickly as you can, but do not jump to a hasty, ill-considered answer.

11) Do not be peremptory in your answers

A brief answer is proper – but do not fire your answer back. That is a losing game from your point of view. The board member can probably ask questions much faster than you can answer them.

12) Do not try to create the answer you think the board member wants

He is interested in what kind of mind you have and how it works – not in playing games. Furthermore, he can usually spot this practice and will actually grade you down on it.

13) Do not switch sides in your reply merely to agree with a board member

Frequently, a member will take a contrary position merely to draw you out and to see if you are willing and able to defend your point of view. Do not start a debate, yet do not surrender a good position. If a position is worth taking, it is worth defending.

14) Do not be afraid to admit an error in judgment if you are shown to be wrong

The board knows that you are forced to reply without any opportunity for careful consideration. Your answer may be demonstrably wrong. If so, admit it and get on with the interview.

15) Do not dwell at length on your present job

The opening question may relate to your present assignment. Answer the question but do not go into an extended discussion. You are being examined for a *new* job, not your present one. As a matter of fact, try to phrase ALL your answers in terms of the job for which you are being examined.

Basis of Rating

Probably you will forget most of these "do's" and "don'ts" when you walk into the oral interview room. Even remembering them all will not ensure you a passing grade. Perhaps you did not have the qualifications in the first place. But remembering them will help you to put your best foot forward, without treading on the toes of the board members.

Rumor and popular opinion to the contrary notwithstanding, an oral board wants you to make the best appearance possible. They know you are under pressure – but they also want to see how you respond to it as a guide to what your reaction would be under the pressures of the job you seek. They will be influenced by the degree of poise you display, the personal traits you show and the manner in which you respond.

ABOUT THIS BOOK

This book contains tests divided into Examination Sections. Go through each test, answering every question in the margin. We have also attached a sample answer sheet at the back of the book that can be removed and used. At the end of each test look at the answer key and check your answers. On the ones you got wrong, look at the right answer choice and learn. Do not fill in the answers first. Do not memorize the questions and answers, but understand the answer and principles involved. On your test, the questions will likely be different from the samples. Questions are changed and new ones added. If you understand these past questions you should have success with any changes that arise. Tests may consist of several types of questions. We have additional books on each subject should more study be advisable or necessary for you. Finally, the more you study, the better prepared you will be. This book is intended to be the last thing you study before you walk into the examination room. Prior study of relevant texts is also recommended. NLC publishes some of these in our Fundamental Series. Knowledge and good sense are important factors in passing your exam. Good luck also helps. So now study this Passbook, absorb the material contained within and take that knowledge into the examination. Then do your best to pass that exam.

EXAMINATION SECTION

EXAMINATION SECTION
TEST 1

DIRECTIONS: Each question or incomplete statement is followed by several suggested answers or completions. Select the one that BEST answers the question or completes the statement. *PRINT THE LETTER OF THE CORRECT ANSWER IN THE SPACE AT THE RIGHT.*

1. Suppose a tenant complains that some of your men are not doing their jobs properly. You should

    A. ask the advice of the assistant resident building superintendent
    B. assume the complaint is correct and report the men responsible
    C. check whether or not the complaint is justified
    D. listen politely, thank him, and forget the matter since the tenant has no authority

    1.____

2. A tenant becomes angry with you because you tell him rules do not allow tenants to go on the roof. You should

    A. explain to him why the rule is necessary
    B. read him the sections of the rules which bar tenants from going on the roof
    C. tell him firmly that you represent the city government
    D. tell him to calm down and you will talk the matter over later

    2.____

3. The BEST way for you to handle an unsociable tenant is to

    A. ask him what he has against you
    B. give him a pleasant greeting anyway
    C. pay no attention to him
    D. tell him your best jokes whenever you see him

    3.____

4. Some older boys are becoming rough while playing in the halls. The BEST way for you to handle this situation is to

    A. call an officer and have them put out
    B. call the manager and have him send someone to help you
    C. pay no attention since their parents would resent your interference
    D. tell them to stop or to go outside to play

    4.____

5. Suppose, while you are on the job, a tenant wishes to pay you for cleaning the hall outside her apartment. This work is a regular part of your crew's daily duties. You should

    A. refuse the money and explain you are paid by the city for doing your job
    B. refuse the money without saying anything further about the matter
    C. take the money and say, "Thank you, very much."
    D. take the money without saying anything further about the matter

    5.____

6. Suppose a tenant asks you to help her find her little boy's ball which has rolled into the basement. You should

    A. explain that you are too busy to be looking for lost balls
    B. help her as a matter of courtesy if it does not take too long
    C. refuse and go on with whatever you are doing
    D. tell her the boy should not have been playing where the ball could be lost

    6.____

1

7. Of the following, the BEST sign that a foreman is doing a good job is if his men

   A. ask his advice when they need it and are able to use it to improve their work
   B. greet him in a friendly manner when they see him
   C. need to ask his advice only when they come across something new on the job
   D. never come to him with grievances

8. One characteristic of a GOOD foreman is that he

   A. asks that his men obey him without question
   B. rarely admits he has made a mistake
   C. realizes that crew meetings are a waste of time
   D. tells his men clearly what he expects of them

9. Of the following, it is MOST important for a foreman to

   A. be able to move rapidly from job to job
   B. be fair to his men
   C. use good English in talking
   D. use good English in writing

10. You would expect a foreman to be *better* than his men in being able to

    A. do their job
    B. do the heavy jobs
    C. train workers in their jobs
    D. work faster at their jobs

11. If a man has been doing a job poorly, telling him so and showing him how to improve is a good way for a foreman to train him to do better work. The foreman should, however, *preferably* do this when

    A. everything else has failed
    B. he is alone with the man
    C. the man is new to the job
    D. the man has made a big mistake

12. When you must talk to a man about some work he has done poorly, it is good at the SAME time to

    A. compare his work with that of one of your best men
    B. mention some of his strong points as well as his faults
    C. offer him a choice of another job
    D. point out previous times when it has been necessary to call him down

13. Usually, the BEST way to teach a caretaker how to do a new job which requires him to use some equipment or tool for the *first* time is by

    A. letting him work it out for himself
    B. showing him how to do it
    C. telling him how to do it
    D. writing out directions

14. The BEST time for a foreman to correct a mistake made by one of his men is   14._____

    A. after the man has learned the job and is on his own
    B. after the man has made the same mistake a few times
    C. as soon as possible after the mistake is made
    D. at the next regular monthly group meeting

15. *Usually*, a foreman should continue training a new man for a job until   15._____

    A. he is satisfied the man knows how to do the job
    B. the man has no more questions about the job
    C. the man has run through the job at least once
    D. the man says he knows how to do the job

16. A foreman could BEST use written instructions to guide his men on how to do a job when   16._____

    A. he wants to make a good showing for his superintendent
    B. he wants to show his men who is boss
    C. one of his men is wasting supplies
    D. there are many steps in the job

17. In training a new man, a mistake that a foreman will *often* make is to   17._____

    A. explain the work so simply the man will lose interest
    B. go from the easy to the harder jobs in explaining the work
    C. show the man how the work should be done instead of telling him
    D. think that the new man knows more than he really does at the start

18. Suppose the foreman is explaining a job to his men and the assistant resident building   18._____
    superintendent, on a tour of inspection, walks over and stops to listen. The foreman
    should

    A. ask the superintendent if he wishes to explain the job himself
    B. call the group to attention
    C. continue to explain the job
    D. explain to the superintendent that some of his men always make a poor showing
       when being watched

19. In disciplining a man, your MOST important aim should be to   19._____

    A. carry out department rules
    B. help train him to be a better employee
    C. keep other men from breaking rules
    D. punish him

20. Of the following, the MAIN value of service ratings, which are used to report regularly on   20._____
    employee's work, is that they

    A. assure that foremen will be fair
    B. reduce complaints about handling pay raises
    C. show the men "how they stand" in their work and why
    D. show where discipline is needed

21. In order to lead his men to look for better methods of doing their work, a foreman should

    A. encourage them to suggest ways for such improvement
    B. point out to them the improvements he has made
    C. try out all changes suggested by the men
    D. try out only those changes suggested by experienced

22. A foreman's orders to his men will *most likely* be followed more willingly if he

    A. explains the reasons behind them
    B. praises those who follow them best
    C. says they are for the good of the department
    D. warns that those who disobey will be fired

23. In requiring his men to obey safety rules, a foreman's stand should be that safety rules MUST be followed because

    A. accident prevention programs were only recently begun in housing projects
    B. a man who follows them need not take any other accident prevention care
    C. they are rules of the department and must be followed without question
    D. they are the result of experience with the best ways of preventing accidents

24. When a foreman was appointed, he told his men about the safety rules they should follow in doing their work.
    About a year later, one of his men was hurt because he did not obey a safety rule.
    On these facts *only*, it can be BEST said that

    A. each man is responsible for his own safety and the safety of the men he works with
    B. telling the men about the safety rules on their first day on the job is sometimes enough
    C. the foreman cannot be held responsible if one of his men does not follow a safety rule
    D. the men should be reminded frequently of safety rules

25. In assigning work to his men, a foreman should realize that

    A. any man can do any job if he gets the proper training
    B. each man is fit for only one kind of job
    C. most men can be taught to do several different kinds of jobs well
    D. the type of job which a man can do best depends more on the foreman than on the man himself

26. Suppose one of your men asks you to assign him to a job for which you do not think he is suited. The BEST thing for you to do is to

    A. assign him to the job since it is better than having a dissatisfied man on your hands
    B. explain why you do not think he is suited for that job
    C. just tell him he cannot have the job without any explanation
    D. tell him you will assign him to the job as soon as possible, hoping he will forget about the matter

27. One of the men comes to you with a complaint about the way you assign men to jobs. You think the matter is unimportant but it seems very important to him and he is excited and angry.
The BEST way for you to handle this situation is to

    A. let him talk until he "gets it off his chest" and then explain the reasons for your assignments
    B. show him at once how unimportant the matter is and how ridiculous his argument is
    C. tell him to wait a few days and you will talk to him when he is cooled off a little
    D. tell him to take the matter up with the assistant superintendent

27.____

28. Suppose, as a new foreman, you are put in charge of a group of men who have been working together for several months. In assigning these men to jobs, you would *probably* get BEST results by

    A. appointing one of the group as the straw boss and holding him responsible for the work of the group
    B. asking them for suggestions for changing jobs
    C. not being influenced by what they have been doing until you find out how well the work is being done
    D. treat them as you would treat any other group

28.____

29. Suppose you have noticed that your men are becoming careless in cleaning halls. It would be BEST to

    A. call together only the men concerned and talk it over with them, telling them they must do better
    B. privately call down each of the men concerned and tell each he must improve
    C. talk the matter over in a general meeting of all your men and mention those who have become careless
    D. talk the matter over in a general meeting of all your men, without mentioning anyone in particular

29.____

30. Suppose you are assigned as a temporary foreman in a housing project over a group of men, some of whom have been in the department and working on the job longer than you have. You feel that these men believe one of them should have been foreman rather than you and they do not like having to "break you in." The BEST way for you to handle this is to

    A. ask the assistant resident buildings supervisor to talk to the men and tell them you are the boss and they must follow your orders
    B. be as "hard boiled" as possible in your dealings with these men in order to show them you are the boss and you are not going to stand for any nonsense
    C. disregard any cases in which these men do not follow the rules in order to show them you are trying to be friendly with them
    D. make a special effort to do an excellent job in every way as a first step in overcoming the opposition of these men

30.____

KEY (CORRECT ANSWERS)

1.	C	16.	D
2.	A	17.	D
3.	B	18.	C
4.	D	19.	B
5.	A	20.	C
6.	B	21.	A
7.	A	22.	A
8.	D	23.	D
9.	B	24.	D
10.	C	25.	C
11.	B	26.	B
12.	B	27.	A
13.	B	28.	D
14.	C	29.	D
15.	A	30.	D

TEST 2

DIRECTIONS: Each question or incomplete statement is followed by several suggested answers or completions. Select the one that BEST answers the question or completes the statement. *PRINT THE LETTER OF THE CORRECT ANSWER IN THE SPACE AT THE RIGHT.*

1. Suppose in the housing project to which you are assigned as a foreman, there is another foreman who, in your opinion, does his work poorly.
   Of the following, the BEST thing for you to do is to

    A. ask to be excused from any jobs in which you will have dealings with the other foreman
    B. carry on your own work properly and say nothing about the work of the other foreman
    C. keep giving the other foreman hints on how to improve his work even though he does not seem to care for your advice
    D. take the matter up with the assistant resident buildings superintendent

    1.____

2. In spite of your efforts, two of your best men do not get along and are always arguing.
   Of the following, the BEST thing you can do is to

    A. keep them on jobs where they do not come together
    B. leave them alone since they are good men
    C. speak to them about how important it is to get along with people
    D. tell them you will have them fired if they do not stop quarreling

    2.____

3. A crew of men without a foreman is sure to run into trouble even in a short time.
   For this reason, it is IMPORTANT that

    A. a foreman never take time off if at all possible
    B. a foreman train and assign a man to take his place when he is absent
    C. every foreman understand every other foreman's job
    D. the crew's work be arranged so that an absent foreman need not be covered

    3.____

4. One of your responsibilities as a foreman is to see that the required work is done on time.
   You can fill this responsibility BEST by

    A. holding weekly meetings with your men to talk over questions
    B. making each man responsible for doing his assigned work
    C. scheduling the work and keeping track of your men as they do it
    D. telling your men how important it is to get the work done on time

    4.____

5. Of the following, the BEST way for a foreman to prevent misuse of supplies is to

    A. give each man instructions as to how to use them best
    B. keep a constant watch over each of his men
    C. keep a record of supplies issued each man and ask anyone using more than the average to explain
    D. tell each man that he will be charged for any waste

    5.____

6. If you want a thing done well, do it yourself.
   This advice CANNOT *always* be followed by a foreman because he

   A. cannot depend on his men
   B. is responsible for all the work of his crew
   C. must assign many jobs to his men
   D. must constantly watch his men

7. The public housing agency employee should think well of his job. His main work is giving protection and service to tenants. We are living in a time when this work is achieving high prestige.
   According to his paragraph,

   A. public opinion towards public housing agencies is becoming less favorable
   B. the main role of all government employees is protection and service
   C. the public housing agency employee is justified in having a high opinion of himself
   D. watching out for a tenant's interests is a large part of a public housing agency employee's work

8. A foreman is the contact man between top management and the worker and it is part of his job to secure obedience to departmental rules through education and training, using discipline only when necessary.
   According to this statement, a foreman should

   A. never use discipline to make his men obey departmental rules
   B. try to get his men to follow departmental rules through understanding
   C. use an equal mixture of education and discipline to get his men to follow departmental rules
   D. use discipline rather than training to get his men to follow departmental rules

9. Good foremen are far more careful than most men in dealing with people. They know that only through other people is it possible to succeed.
   According to this statement,

   A. a good foreman gives other people what they want
   B. good foremen recognize the importance of their relations with other people
   C. it takes an educated man to be a good foreman
   D. those who are careful in dealing with other people will be good foremen

10. Intelligence is not the only requirement of the successful foreman. He must be honest and industrious.
    According to this statement, a successful foreman MUST be

    A. able to handle difficult problems
    B. as intelligent as he is honest
    C. honest and industrious as well as intelligent
    D. loyal under all circumstances

11. A foreman who is open-minded and alert can learn something every time a man comes to him with a grievance. This is especially true if the foreman is big enough to accept responsibility for his own mistakes and to see the viewpoint of the man who brings up the grievance.
    According to this statement, when he deals with grievances,

A. a foreman who is open-minded and alert will learn how to avoid them
B. a foreman should accept responsibility for the mistakes his men make
C. the most important thing for the foreman to consider is the good of the department
D. it is important for the foreman to understand the worker's side of the grievance

12. A foreman's continuous checking of the work of his men will keep it safe and up to standard but it will also hinder its rapid finish. This continuous checking serves the cause of order but not of speed.
According to this statement,

    A. a foreman's continuous check on the work of his men, while serving a useful purpose, also has a disadvantage
    B. a foreman must choose between doing a job slowly or in a safe and orderly manner
    C. speedy completion of a job is always to be desired even if other things must be sacrificed
    D. there can be no rapid completion of a job unless all checking is done away with

13. A foreman's records form the memory of his organization, and the speed with which they can be made available is important in getting the job done. Even in a small group, the memory of the foreman or any of his men cannot safely be depended upon to be correct and complete, and therefore, his records must be used.
According to this statement,

    A. a foreman's memory is not as good as his records for accurate and complete information
    B. a good memory will give a foreman correct and complete information about his crew
    C. records are not necessary if there is a foreman or caretaker in the crew with a good memory
    D. records are of no use at all unless they are absolutely correct and complete

14. A foreman should never fail to recognize that his men have a perfect right to come to him with their grievances. In fact, that is an important part of every foreman's job. That is why people are placed in foreman positions so that the men can come to them with questions, complaints, suggestions, and for information. Disagreements and hurt feelings always arise whenever men work together.
According to this statement,

    A. a good foreman can correct conditions before grievances develop
    B. a man with "a chip on his shoulder" should not be allowed to come to a foreman with a grievance
    C. grievances cannot be avoided whenever men work together
    D. settling grievances is the most important part of a foreman's job

15. Sometimes in doing his work, a foreman must act alone, without advice from his assistant superintendent, and without any department manuals or books to guide him.
This statement means that a foreman, in doing his work, must *sometimes* be

    A. active   B. cautious
    C. self-reliant   D. stern-faced

QUESTIONS 16-25.

Questions 16 to 25 refer to the foreman's time sheet for his crew for one week. The hours worked each day or the reason the man was off on that day are shown on the sheet. "R" means rest day, "A" means annual leave, "S" means sick leave. Where a man worked only part of a day, both the number of hours worked and the number of hours taken off are entered. The reason for absence is entered in parentheses next to the number of hours taken off. Questions 16 to 25 are to be answered *solely* on the information in the time sheet.

Name	Saturday	Sunday	Monday	Tuesday	Wednesday	Thursday	Friday
Smith	R	R	7	7	7	3 4(A)	7
Jones	R	7	7	7	7	7	R
Green	R	R	7	7	S	S	S
White	R	R	7	7	A	7	7
Doe	7	7	7	7	7	R	R
Brown	R	R	A	7	7	7	7
Black	R	R	S	7	7	7	7
Reed	R	R	7	7	7	7	S
Roe	R	R	A	7	7	7	7
Lane	7	R	R	7	7	A	S

16. The caretaker who worked *exactly* 21 hours during the week is

    A. Lane   B. Roe
    C. Smith   D. White

17. The *total* number of hours worked by ALL caretakers during the week is

    A. 268   B. 276   C. 280   D. 288

18. The two days of the week on which MOST caretakers were off are

    A. Thursday and Friday   B. Friday and Saturday
    C. Saturday and Sunday   D. Sunday and Monday

19. The day on which three caretakers were off on sick leave is

    A. Monday   B. Friday
    C. Saturday   D. Sunday

20. The two workers who took LEAST time off during the week are

    A. Doe and Reed   B. Jones and Doe
    C. Reed and Smith   D. Smith and Jones

21. The caretaker who worked the LEAST number of hours during the week is

    A. Brown   B. Green   C. Lane   D. Roe

22. The caretakers who did NOT work on Thursday are

    A. Doe, White, and Smith   B. Green, Doe, and Lane
    C. Green, Doe, and Smith   D. Green, Lane, and Smith

23. The day on which one caretaker worked *only* three hours is 23._____

    A. Friday B. Saturday
    C. Thursday D. Wednesday

24. The day on which ALL caretakers worked is 24._____

    A. Friday B. Thursday
    C. Tuesday D. Wednesday

25. The AVERAGE number of hours per day that each caretaker worked is closest to 25._____

    A. 25 B. 28 C. 29 D. 31

KEY (CORRECT ANSWERS)

1. B   11. D
2. A   12. A
3. B   13. A
4. C   14. C
5. A   15. C

6. C   16. A
7. D   17. B
8. B   18. C
9. B   19. B
10. C 20. B

21. B
22. B
23. C
24. C
25. B

EXAMINATION SECTION
TEST 1

DIRECTIONS: Each question or incomplete statement is followed by several suggested answers or completions. Select the one that BEST answers the question or completes the statement. *PRINT THE LETTER OF THE CORRECT ANSWER IN THE SPACE AT THE RIGHT.*

1. Which of the following substances causes asphalt tile to turn spongy? 1._____

    A. Oil   B. Varnish   C. Water   D. Dust

2. Which of the following would NOT cause asphalt tile to turn yellow? 2._____

    A. A layer of dust   B. Varnish
    C. Lacquer   D. Water

3. Which one of the following is LEAST likely to be an advantage of waxing a floor? 3._____

    A. Helps to make a room quieter
    B. Helps to reduce wear on the floor
    C. Gives a pleasant shine to the floor
    D. Improves the stain resistance of the floor

4. The action of liquid cleaner on a floor with built-up wax is to 4._____

    A. make the wax disappear into the air
    B. turn the wax into little grains that must be swept up in a vacuum cleaner
    C. soften the wax, which has to be scrubbed away and then rinsed off
    D. make the floor waterproof

5. After how many waxings should built-up wax be removed from a floor? 5._____
    Every

    A. waxing   B. 3 waxings
    C. 6 waxings   D. 12 waxings

6. Manuals on floor cleaning describe methods of cleaning *resilient flooring*. 6._____
    Which of the following kinds of flooring surfaces is NOT *resilient*?
    _____ tile.

    A. Cork   B. Asphalt   C. Vinyl   D. Terrazzo

7. In buffing a floor, it is NOT desirable to use a polishing brush because the 7._____

    A. brush will scratch the surface you are trying to polish
    B. strands of the brush fall out easily
    C. brush is often used for other purposes
    D. brush does not usually remove deep scuff marks

8. *Rolling* results when only the upper parts of a wax coat dry, leaving the lower parts wet. 8._____
    In waxing a floor, this condition comes from

    A. putting on too thick a coat of wax
    B. putting on too thin a coat of wax

C. rinsing the floor before applying the wax
D. leaving soap on the floor before applying the wax

9. After a cork or linoleum floor is installed, how long should you wait before you mop the floor for the FIRST time?

   A. 1 day B. 3 days C. 12 hours D. 2 weeks

10. On sweeping stairways, you should direct your men to make a practice of sweeping them

    A. when tenant traffic is heavy, so that people can see them working
    B. whenever they have free time during the day
    C. during the morning at a time when tenant traffic is lightest
    D. in the middle of the day, when the traffic is medium heavy

11. How often must public corridors be swept?

    A. Only when a visible amount of dirt piles up
    B. Every day
    C. Once a week
    D. Every three days

12. You should NOT use an oily mop to sweep any floor because it

    A. leaves a sticky film that can catch dust
    B. eats away at the floor like acid
    C. makes the floor completely waterproof
    D. prevents wax from being applied

13. Which of the following would NOT be used on a concrete floor?

    A. Water base wax   B. Oily sweeping compound
    C. Solvent wax   D. Wire brush

14. You should NOT use an alkaline cleaner on linoleum floors because the cleaner

    A. will make the floor shine too brightly
    B. makes the linoleum sticky
    C. makes the linoleum crack and curl
    D. costs too much to be practical

15. The BEST way of wet mopping a large floor area is to mop the floor area

    A. with a circular motion
    B. from side to side or with a figure 8 motion
    C. with forward and back strokes
    D. alternate side to side and forward and back

16. The type of product to use when cleaning terrazzo floors is

    A. mild cleaner   B. diluted acid solution
    C. scouring powder   D. paste wax

17. A caretaker was met mopping an asphalt tile floor. He decided to make the floor as wet as possible.
    For him to do this is a

    A. *good* idea, because the more water you use, the cleaner the floor will be
    B. *bad* idea, because water should never be wasted
    C. *good* idea, because the floor will not have to be washed as often
    D. *bad* idea, because the excess water will eventually damage the floor surface

18. When you wet clean a stairway by hand, you need two buckets.
    One of them is for the cleaning solution, and the other one is used for

    A. extra ammonia for cleaning
    B. rinsing, and should be filled with clean water
    C. putting out fires, and should be filled with sand
    D. storage of equipment

19. The cleaning of stairways is USUALLY scheduled to be done with

    A. corridor cleaning   B. sidewalk cleaning
    C. incinerator work   D. move-outs

20. *Dry cleaning* in relation to a building refers to

    A. a reconditioning process that restores the appearance of a floor and protects the surface by buffing
    B. dusting of a wall area with specially treated cloth in order to produce a sheen
    C. patch waxing of a floor with a powdered wax compound
    D. dry mopping only of a floor area

Questions 21-25.

DIRECTIONS: Questions 21 through 25 are to be answered ONLY according to the information given in the following paragraph.

In order to help prevent the spread of fire, it is necessary to understand the means by which heat is transmitted. Heat is transmitted through solids by a method called *conduction*. Materials vary greatly in their ability to transmit heat. Metals are good conductors of heat. On the other hand, wood, glass, pottery, asbestos, and many like substances are very poor conductors of heat and are termed insulators. It should be remembered, however, that there are no perfect insulators of heat. All will conduct heat to some extent, and if the heat continues long enough, it will be transmitted through the solid. The hazard of heat transmission is illustrated by the fact that a fire on one side of a metal wall could start a fire on the other side if combustibles were close to the wall.

21. Of the following, the BEST material to use for the handle of a metal pan to guard against heat is

    A. copper   B. iron   C. wood   D. steel

22. According to the above paragraph, *conduction* applies to the traveling of heat through a

    A. solid   B. liquid
    C. slow-moving fluid   D. gas

23. According to the information in the above paragraph, when storing combustible materials in a room with metal walls, it is BEST to

    A. keep the combustibles close together
    B. keep the combustibles away from the metal walls
    C. put the non-metals nearest the metal walls
    D. separate metal materials from non-metal materials

24. Based on the information in the above paragraph, which one of the following objects is the BEST conductor of heat?

    A. Pottery   B. An oak desk
    C. A glass jar   D. A silver spoon

25. Of the following, the title which BEST describes what the above paragraph is about is

    A. Uses of Conductors and Insulators
    B. The Reasons Why Fire Spreads
    C. Heat Transmission and Fires
    D. The Hazards of Poor Conduction

KEY (CORRECT ANSWERS)

1.	A	11.	B
2.	A	12.	A
3.	A	13.	B
4.	C	14.	C
5.	C	15.	B
6.	D	16.	A
7.	D	17.	D
8.	A	18.	B
9.	B	19.	A
10.	C	20.	A

21. C
22. A
23. B
24. D
25. C

TEST 2

DIRECTIONS: Each question or incomplete statement is followed by several suggested answers or completions. Select the one that BEST answers the question or completes the statement. *PRINT THE LETTER OF THE CORRECT ANSWER IN THE SPACE AT THE RIGHT.*

1. If it is necessary to wash stairways, this should be done during the

   A. day
   B. night
   C. weekend
   D. morning rush hour

   1.____

2. A caretaker noticed that a family was moving out. He gave the following information to the foreman: name and apartment number of the family and the van license number. Which one of the following facts did the caretaker leave out that he should have given to the foreman?

   A. Registration number of the moving van
   B. Inspection date of the moving van
   C. Name of the moving company
   D. Names and addresses of the movers

   2.____

3. A caretaker sees that a lock on the outside door of a project building has been broken by vandals.
   This should be reported FIRST to the

   A. housing manager
   B. foreman of caretakers
   C. building superintendent
   D. assistant building superintendent

   3.____

4. In housing authority practice, a garage broom is *usually* used to sweep

   A. small asphalt walks
   B. playgrounds
   C. small cement walks
   D. incinerator rooms

   4.____

5. Listed below, and numbered in scrambled order, are the first four steps to follow when you are dusting furniture:
   - I. Move objects on furniture and dust under them
   - II. Refold cloth
   - III. Dust furniture itself
   - IV. Fold the dusting cloth

   The CORRECT order of these steps should be:

   A. I, IV, III, II
   B. III, IV, II, I
   C. IV, II, I, III
   D. IV, III, II, I

   5.____

6. Snow removal should begin

   A. after the snow has been packed solid
   B. as soon as possible
   C. when the depth is more than 2 inches
   D. when the weather bureau says it is a *heavy snowfall*

   6.____

7. On which of the following should you advise a caretaker to use a corn broom?

   A. Basement areas B. Stair halls
   C. Rubber tile floor D. Window sills

8. Chrome fixtures should be cleaned by

   A. using a mild soap solution then polishing with a soft cloth
   B. dusting lightly, then wax with oil base wax
   C. polishing with a scouring pad
   D. washing with a solution of water and ammonia, then rinsing with a detergent

9. The MAIN reason caretakers are advised to wear protective goggles while changing a broken bulb is to avoid the danger of

   A. glare from the bulb
   B. pieces of glass getting in the eyes
   C. sparks from the bulb
   D. insects on or around the bulb socket

10. Oily rags should be placed in a container made of

    A. metal B. cardboard
    C. cloth D. wood

11. When a caretaker lights an incinerator in the morning, the door to the incinerator room should be

    A. all the way open
    B. all the way closed
    C. half-way open, to let the air in
    D. open or closed, depending on the weather

12. Wood and cork floors should be sealed because

    A. these surfaces have tiny natural openings that can trap dirt and grease
    B. it keeps these kinds of floors from warping and buckling
    C. it makes the surface stronger
    D. the sealing process makes the surface easier to walk on

13. A single 8-foot ladder is to be used for a certain window washing job. Of the distances from the wall which are given below, which one is BEST to place the ladder from the wall? _____ feet.

    A. 2   B. 4   C. 6   D. 8

14. To lift something without injury to yourself, you should obey all of the following rules EXCEPT:

    A. Keep your back straight
    B. Get help with heavy loads
    C. Lift quickly with your arms
    D. Stand close to what you are lifting

15. The type of product to use when cleaning asphalt tile is 15.____

    A. sandpaper pad B. plain ammonia
    C. water base wax D. oil base polish

16. When you are taking a mop outfit with wringer through a corridor, it is VERY important to proceed slowly past doorways because 16.____

    A. you might slip and hurt yourself
    B. you should look for any cracks in the floor
    C. you must watch out for people who might come through the doorway
    D. the doorway area is more slippery than the rest of the corridor

17. Which one of the following is the MOST important piece of clothing to wear while cleaning an incinerator? 17.____

    A. Leather boots B. Fireman's helmet
    C. Heavy coat D. Work gloves

18. Of the following, who should hang the elevator pads to be used when tenants move in or out? 18.____
    The

    A. foreman of housing caretakers
    B. tenant himself
    C. caretaker assigned to the building
    D. elevator mechanic

19. One day a caretaker said to his foreman, *I can get a tile cleaner that is as good as the stuff we use, and for less money, because my brother is a building contractor. How about it?* 19.____
    The CORRECT way for the foreman to handle this situation is for him to

    A. thank the caretaker, but tell him that individual caretakers cannot buy their own cleaning material for project use
    B. tell the caretaker that no one has any right to start interfering in the buying procedures of the housing authority
    C. go along with the caretaker and buy the cleaner from his brother, because it might save money for the authority
    D. tell the caretaker to have his brother contact the project manager

20. A new caretaker under your supervision is waxing a floor for the first time. While the job seems to be going along well, he is not doing it quite the way you asked him to do it and so is taking longer than he should. 20.____
    Which of the following is the BEST action for you to take under these conditions?

    A. Leave him to finish the job and go on to the next one
    B. Interrupt him and tell him to do the job the way he was taught
    C. Tell him he is doing well but that he should do better
    D. Explain to him why your way is faster and tell him to try it

21. The EASIEST way to find out how many supplies you have available is for you to 21.____

    A. look at last year's figures
    B. keep an up-to-date inventory

C. ask one of your men to let you know
D. check the availability when you use a special item

Questions 22-23.

DIRECTIONS: Questions 22 and 23 are to be answered on the basis of information in the following paragraph.

Studies show that the average high-class office building has a tenant population of around 750 persons per 100,000 square feet of area and that the elevators normally have to handle from seven to ten times as many passengers per day as the total number of permanent occupants.

22. Based on the above, what would be the AVERAGE tenant population of a building having 300,000 square feet of space?

   A. 1,000   B. 2,250   C. 2,200   D. 750

23. Based on the above, how many passengers would the elevator have to handle per day if the area of the building is 100,000 square feet?
   From

   A. 5,250 to 7,500   B. 750 to 1,500
   C. 1,000 to 2,500   D. 2,500 to 5,000

Questions 24-25.

DIRECTIONS: Questions 24 and 25 are to be answered on the basis of information in the paragraph below.

A large number of studies show that in diversified tenancy buildings, the maximum five-minute morning incoming traffic flow averages 12% of the building population and that the noon peak at its highest five-minute period averages about 15% of the building, population.

24. Based on the above, with a building population of 1,000, how many people would the elevators have to handle during the MAXIMUM incoming morning traffic period?

   A. 120   B. 130   C. 150   D. 160

25. How many people during the highest five-minute peak period of the noon rush hour would the elevator be able to handle at MAXIMUM capacity with a building population of 1,000?

   A. 120   B. 125   C. 150   D. 175

KEY (CORRECT ANSWERS)

1.	C	11.	B
2.	C	12.	A
3.	B	13.	A
4.	B	14.	C
5.	D	15.	C
6.	B	16.	C
7.	A	17.	D
8.	A	18.	C
9.	B	19.	A
10.	A	20.	D

21. B
22. B
23. A
24. A
25. C

EXAMINATION SECTION
TEST 1

DIRECTIONS: Each question or incomplete statement is followed by several suggested answers or completions. Select the one that BEST answers the question or completes the statement. *PRINT THE LETTER OF THE CORRECT ANSWER IN THE SPACE AT THE RIGHT.*

1. A foreman will MOST likely be respected by his men if he

    A. keeps his personnel records simple and clear
    B. offers them advice in solving their family problems
    C. leaves it to them to decide how a job is to be done
    D. is fair and honest with them

2. When a foreman assigns work to his men, it is usually BEST for him to

    A. give each man the same amount of work
    B. give the jobs that take the longest time to the senior men
    C. assign work to each man according to his ability
    D. let each man pick his own assignment

3. When a new caretaker comes on the job, it is LEAST important for him to know

    A. the location of the buildings in the project
    B. how long you have been the foreman
    C. the names of the men he will work with
    D. where to pick up tools and equipment

4. When a foreman has to teach a man a new job, it would be MOST helpful for him to find out

    A. how long the man has been with the department and how long he plans to stay
    B. the man's dependability and willingness
    C. the man's past record of cooperation with other workers
    D. what the man already knows that will help him in learning the new job

5. Suppose that a new type waxing machine is to be used in your project. Of the following, the BEST way for you to teach your men how to use this machine is to

    A. give a talk on how to operate the machine
    B. demonstrate the operation and then have each man operate the machine under your supervision
    C. have the manufacturer give a talk on how to operate the machine
    D. give each man a set of carefully written instructions on how to operate the machine

6. Suppose that as a foreman you have finished *breaking in* a new employee. A few days later, you see the man doing the job the wrong way. You should

    A. immediately show the man what he is doing wrong and how to do it correctly
    B. assign him to some other work
    C. let your superior know that the new man cannot follow instructions
    D. say nothing because you may make the new man nervous

7. Suppose that the department is introducing a new procedure for cleaning the hallways of project buildings. As a foreman, the BEST way for you to acquaint your men with this new procedure and to get them to use it is to

   A. wait until it has been tried out in another project and, if it is successful, put it into use in your project
   B. give each man a printed copy of the new procedure, and set a deadline date by which each man is to read it and know it
   C. get your men together and explain the new procedure to them and how it will affect their work
   D. teach it to your best man and when he is familiar with it ask him to teach it to the other men one at a time

7.____

8. One of your experienced workers and a new employee are arguing about the correct way to do a job on which they are working together. As the foreman, you should

   A. listen to both men and then tell them that they must learn to settle their argument without interrupting your work
   B. side with the older worker because he is more experienced
   C. listen to both men and then tell them how the work is to be done
   D. take one of the men off the job

8.____

9. Suppose that one of your men who is doing good work asks for a transfer to another foreman. It would be BEST for you to

   A. have a private talk with the man to find out why he wants a transfer
   B. tell the man that the other foreman will also expect him to do good work
   C. approve the transfer without question because a dissatisfied man will do a poor job
   D. ask the other men in your crew if they are dissatisfied with your supervision

9.____

10. Because of absences, a foreman is short-handed. Which one of the following operations should he lay over so that he can cover the MOST important work on a minimum basis?

    A. Incineration of garbage
    B. Sweeping the lobby
    C. Sweeping and washing the elevators
    D. Washing corridor windows

10.____

11. At a quarter to five, one of your employees tells you that the incinerator in his building has much refuse in it and he is willing to work overtime to burn it. If you give him permission to do this, it would be

    A. *good,* because it will save time the next day for other important work
    B. *bad,* because this is not an emergency for which overtime could be approved
    C. *good,* because tenants would not complain that refuse piles up and causes odors
    D. *bad,* because the law does not allow burning after 5:00 P.M.

11.____

12. When he discusses a grievance with an employee, the foreman should

    A. not tell the employee what he thinks of his complaint until a later date
    B. avoid any arguments with the employee
    C. convince the employee that there is no basis for this grievance
    D. tell the employee his complaint is justified

12.____

13. Suppose that your men were asked to work overtime in order to repair a water main break. When the work is finished, the manager thanks you for the excellent work that was done. For you, as foreman, to tell your men about this would be

    A. *bad,* because this was a private conversation between you and your superior
    B. *good,* because your men will see that you are well liked by the manager
    C. *bad,* because your men will think that they will be asked to work whenever there is an emergency
    D. *good,* because it will show the men their cooperation is appreciated

14. Suppose that you and your supervisor are making an inspection of one of the buildings you are responsible for cleaning. Your superior notices that the elevator in the building has not been cleaned. You know that a new employee who has been on the job for only three months is assigned to this building. You should

    A. tell your supervisor that you will have the elevator cleaned and see that it is kept clean in the future
    B. explain to your supervisor the trouble you have in training new employees
    C. find the new man and ask him to explain to you and your superior why the elevator is not clean
    D. tell your supervisor that the elevator was clean when you made your last inspection

15. One of your men makes a suggestion for improving the method of doing the work. You don't think the suggestion is workable. As foreman, you should

    A. forget the idea since it isn't workable
    B. tell the man to try out the idea and hold him responsible if it doesn't work out
    C. discuss with the man why you think the idea won't work and praise him for his interest in the job
    D. point out to the man that he is wasting your time bringing up an idea that is not practical

16. Suppose you are a new foreman and you are put in charge of a gang of men whom you do not know and who have been working together for a few months. For a smooth changeover to your leadership, it would be BEST for you to

    A. let them continue working at their present assignments while you get to know them better
    B. tell the men to call their old foreman if they have any trouble while you are learning the job
    C. ask the most experienced man to take charge of the gang for a short while until you are more familiar with the work
    D. ask each man whether he is satisfied with what he is doing or wants a change

17. Two of your men start an argument while at work. As their foreman, you should

    A. ignore them; it is normal for men working together to have arguments
    B. stop them right away and find out what started the argument
    C. let them argue it out as long as they continue working and don't talk too loud
    D. speak to one of the men privately and tell him he is interfering with the work

18. One of your men complains about a job you gave him. He is angry about getting the assignment. You don't think that the man is right in getting so upset. You should

    A. discuss the problem with him and explain why you gave him the job
    B. refer the man to your supervisor because he refuses to obey orders
    C. show the man that the whole matter is unimportant and a waste of time
    D. tell the man to do the job first and complain later

19. Suppose that you are a foreman and one of your men is absent from work one day. You don't have any extra men, and some of the work usually done by the absent man has to be finished that day. It would be BEST for you to

    A. call your men together and let them decide which one is to do the work
    B. shorten the lunch period and have each man do some of the work
    C. ask one of your better men to *pitch in* by doing a little extra work today
    D. explain to the buildings superintendent why it will not be possible to finish this work today

20. Suppose you are a foreman and one of your men asks why you did not recommend him for an above average work performance rating. You should tell him

    A. that above average work reports can be recommended only by higher authority
    B. why you did not give him an above average work report
    C. that you will recommend an above average work performance rating next year if he does better work
    D. how he can appeal his rating and help him write his appeal

21. It is MOST important that a report from a foreman to his superior be

    A. typewritten
    B. free of any mistakes in spelling or English
    C. accurate and have all the necessary facts
    D. brief to save time of all concerned

22. Assume that you are a foreman and have to write a report on a new employee who will finish his probationary period next month. Which one of the following would be the BEST reason for recommending that he be dropped from the job?
    He

    A. was late several times during the past five months for a total of 50 minutes
    B. is a slow worker compared to the other men
    C. insists on eating his lunch alone instead of with the other men
    D. is in the habit of accepting drinks from tenants during working hours although you have often told him it is forbidden

23. A requisition would be filled out by a foreman in order to

    A. get supplies from the stockroom
    B. return to the stockroom supplies he hasn't used
    C. find out the supplies he has on hand
    D. show that supplies were used up faster than expected

24. As foreman, your attitude to complaints by tenants should be that

    A. all tenants like to complain
    B. if you let the tenant *give off some steam* the complaint will disappear
    C. you will listen to them and try to correct the condition where the need is indicated
    D. you will try to show the tenant where he is wrong

25. As you start work one morning, you notice a moving van partly loaded with household furniture parked in front of a project building. Although you have no official notice of any *move out* scheduled for that day, a tenant you know seems to be moving out of her apartment. As a foreman, your FIRST action should be to

    A. have the caretaker hang up the elevator pads right away
    B. write down the truck's license number and name of the moving company
    C. talk to the tenant and, without arousing her suspicion, find out her new address
    D. call a patrolman to stop the tenant from moving

26. Of the following, the BEST reason for NOT allowing the department employees to accept tips from people is that

    A. all employees would not be given equal treatment
    B. employees would become dishonest
    C. people are entitled to service without tips
    D. people in projects can't afford tips

27. If a person asks you to do some work for her which you are not allowed to do, you should

    A. ask her to speak to the manager
    B. explain to her why you can't do the work
    C. offer to do it on your day off
    D. report the person to the management office

28. A person who has lost her key asks you to unlock her door with a pass key. You should

    A. tell her she must first let the management office know that she is locked out
    B. open the door as a matter of courtesy
    C. refer her to the patrolman who has the authority in such matters
    D. ask her where she lost the key and help her look for it

29. A person complains to you that she saw an employee wasting water while he was mopping a hall. The person is annoyed because she has heard of the appeal to save water because of the water shortage. As foreman, you should

    A. take her to the assistant superintendent so she can tell him what she saw
    B. listen to her patiently and ask her why she didn't stop the employee from wasting water
    C. thank her for her interest and tell her you'll speak to the employee
    D. have her point out the employee and while she listens give the man a talk on saving water

30. While you are working in a tenant's apartment, she begins to argue with her son about his staying out late at night on school days. You feel that the mother is right. You should

    A. tell them to stop arguing or you will have to report them to the management office
    B. say nothing, even though you believe the mother is right, and leave the apartment if the argument continues
    C. tell them to finish their argument in another room as they are interfering with your work
    D. get a patrolman to stop the argument

31. While making your rounds, you see a group of teenagers running around the playground area in the project and teasing the smaller children playing there. As foreman, you should

    A. get the names of the teenagers and turn them in to the management office
    B. continue on your rounds as the playground isn't in your area of supervision
    C. have the mothers take the small children out of the playground
    D. ask the teenagers to stop because they may hurt the younger children

32. Tenants are not allowed to keep paper cartons in the basement storage room of a project building MAINLY because

    A. the cartons are a fire hazard
    B. the limited space should be used only for storing large, bulky items
    C. articles can be stolen easily from paper cartons
    D. storage rooms below ground level are usually damp and easily flooded

33. A respirator should be used to

    A. sweep the inside corridors of a project building
    B. mop a large floor area with ammonia
    C. clean the incinerator settling chamber
    D. clean landscaped areas on a windy day

34. The BEST time for cleaning the elevators in a project apartment building is between 9 and 10 in the morning because

    A. the elevators can be taken out of service temporarily without too much inconvenience to the tenants
    B. passenger traffic is usually heavy at this time
    C. move-ins and move-outs are not permitted during this time
    D. the morning air will help to dry out the elevator quickly

35. The BEST way to wash dirty brooms and brushes is with

    A. cold clear water
    B. warm water and detergent
    C. cold water and soap flakes
    D. warm water and ammonia

36. The expression *cutting the water,* as used in washing windows, means

    A. tilting the squeegee so that about 2 inches of the rubber touches the glass
    B. adding ammonia to the water to cut through the dirt on the window

C. soaking up the water at the bottom of the window with a sponge
D. using chemicals to increase the wetting power of the water

37. To remove wax crayon marks from brick and cement walls, the department recommends a mixture of   37._____

    A. carbon tetrachloride and soap powder
    B. paint thinner and wood alcohol
    C. trisodium phosphate and ammonia
    D. synthetic detergent and turpentine

38. For sweeping a wet or rough surface, you should NEVER use a   38._____

    A. corn broom   B. deck brush
    C. garage broom   D. hair broom

39. The BEST way to remove the stiffness from a new corn broom before using it for the first time is to   39._____

    A. comb out the straws with a tampico brush
    B. store the broom in a damp closet overnight
    C. soak the broom in water overnight
    D. stand the broom on end overnight

40. Use water sparingly on mopping tile floors of linoleum or rubber. The MOST important reason for this is that   40._____

    A. too much water will spot the floor
    B. soap loses its cleaning power when there is too much water
    C. the tiles will come loose if too much water gets under them
    D. it takes more time to mop the floor when more water is used

41. The baked enamel walls of an elevator cab should NEVER be cleaned with a solution of water and   41._____

    A. ammonia   B. detergent
    C. disinfectant   D. lemon oil

42. Dust and sweepings from stairways should NOT be dropped into the incinerator hopper MAINLY because they   42._____

    A. may be blown back into the hall by the draft
    B. will remain suspended in the incinerator chute
    C. will put out the fire in the incinerator
    D. may cause an explosion

43. The proper equipment to use when removing the broken end of a light bulb from a socket is   43._____

    A. gloves, wedge, and goggles
    B. bulb changer, screwdriver, and goggles
    C. putty knife, goggles, and screwdriver
    D. bulb changer, long-nose pliers, and gloves

44. To clean brass lacquer coated mail boxes, the proper agent to use is   44._____

    A. a mild soap solution
    B. a brass polish
    C. lemon oil and #00 steel wool
    D. soft rags with mild scouring powder

45. Which one of the following statements about tile is NOT correct?   45._____
    Glazed tile

    A. is easier to keep clean than unglazed tile
    B. does not have to be wiped after it is washed but unglazed tile must be wiped
    C. has a smoother and harder surface than unglazed tile
    D. tends to show water streaks while unglazed tile will not streak

46. Suppose that because of a flue stoppage between the third and fourth floor hoppers, there is insufficient draft for the incinerator. Which of the following is the POOREST method for clearing the flue?   46._____

    A. Drop a heavy weight through the fourth floor hopper
    B. Clean the spark arrester screen on the roof if it is blocked
    C. Light a piece of newspaper and toss it into the incinerator firebox
    D. Set fire to the refuse from the floor above the stoppage

47. Although most employees know the safety precautions to take in doing a job, they too often have a tendency to disregard these precautions so that they themselves are largely responsible for accidents which occur.   47._____
    According to this statement, accidents MOST often happen because employees

    A. misunderstand safety instructions
    B. neglect to follow safety rules
    C. lack experience on the job
    D. receive insufficient training from their supervisors

48. When a foreman investigates an accident in the project either to a tenant or to one of his men, his MAIN purpose should be to   48._____

    A. find out if the man should be brought up on charges
    B. find out if the tenant should be made to move out
    C. get the facts and learn how to prevent such accidents
    D. prove that the department was not to blame

49. Which one of the following statements about the soda-acid fire extinguisher is CORRECT?   49._____
    It

    A. should not be used on electrical fires
    B. does not have to be protected from freezing temperatures
    C. will quickly put out a paint or oil fire
    D. requires a fresh soda-acid change every month

50. When a 12 foot ladder is set against a wall for working on it, how far should the bottom of   50._____
    the ladder be from the base of the wall?
    _____ feet.
    A. 2   B. 3   C. 5   D. 6

KEY (CORRECT ANSWERS)

1. D	11. D	21. C	31. D	41. D
2. C	12. B	22. D	32. A	42. D
3. B	13. D	23. A	33. C	43. A
4. D	14. A	24. C	34. A	44. A
5. B	15. C	25. B	35. B	45. D
6. A	16. A	26. C	36. A	46. C
7. C	17. B	27. B	37. C	47. B
8. C	18. A	28. A	38. D	48. C
9. A	19. C	29. C	39. C	49. A
10. D	20. B	30. B	40. C	50. B

TEST 2

DIRECTIONS: Each question or incomplete statement is followed by several suggested answers or completions. Select the one that BEST answers the question or completes the statement. *PRINT THE LETTER OF THE CORRECT ANSWER IN THE SPACE AT THE RIGHT.*

1. On which one of the following screw heads would you use a Phillips screwdriver?   1.____

A. 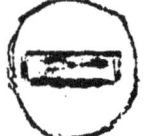   B.    C.    D.

2.   2.____

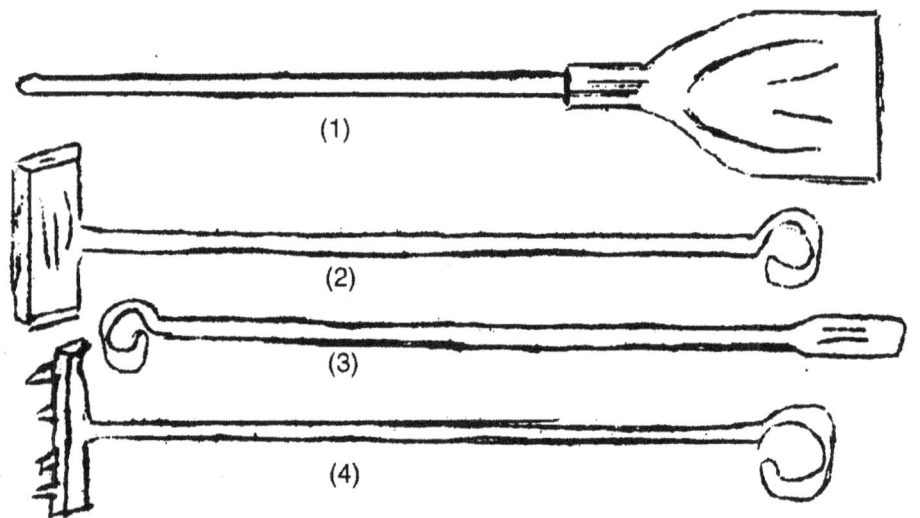

The CORRECT names for the incinerator tools shown above are: (1) _____, (2) _____, (3) _____, (4) _____.

A. shovel; rake; hoe; slicer
B. shovel; ash cutter; poker; rake
C. shovel; hoe; spear; fan rake
D. shovel; hoe; slice bar; rake

Questions 3-7.

DIRECTIONS: Choose from Column II the BEST broom or brush to use for each sweeping job in Questions 3 through 7.

COLUMN I	COLUMN II	
3. Sweeping inside stairhalls and corridors	A. 	3._____
4. Sweeping small outside cement and asphalt walks	B. 	4._____
5. Sweeping small inside areas such as window sills, corners, and stairs	C. 	5._____
6. Sweeping large outside cement or asphalt areas such as playgrounds	D. 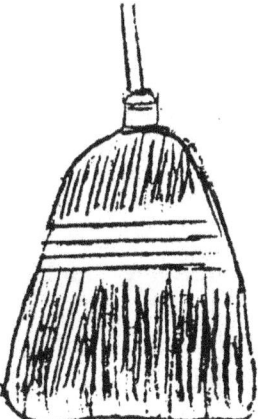	6._____
7. Sweeping dust and small rubbish from the floor onto a dust pan		7._____

8. A ladder should NOT be painted MAINLY because paint   8._____

   A. may hide cracks in the wood
   B. is expensive
   C. prevents the wood from aging properly
   D. would make the steps slippery

9. If a ladder being used for work has a cracked rung, the foreman should   9._____

   A. glue the rung immediately with a good epoxy cement
   B. warn his men not to step on the cracked rung
   C. put the ladder away and get another one
   D. take the ladder out of service when the work is finished and make out a repair order the same day

10. When lifting a heavy object from the floor, it is NOT a good practice to   10._____

    A. bend the knees and keep the back straight
    B. lift slowly
    C. spread the feet slightly, with one foot in front of the other
    D. use the arm muscles more than the leg muscles

11. When a waxing machine plugged into a wall outlet in a hall is operated, the motor stops right away and the hall lights go out. This would indicate that   11._____

    A. a higher rated fuse should be installed in the fuse box
    B. the hall lights and the wall outlet are on the same circuit
    C. the tenants in the line over the outlet are using too many electrical appliances
    D. the wall outlet has a loose connection

12. An employee should be instructed that when he carries mops, buckets, brooms, and similar materials up a stairway, he should   12._____

    A. carry something in each hand in order to keep good balance
    B. climb the stairs slowly so that he can carry everything in one trip
    C. have another employee stand at the bottom of the stairway to catch anything he drops
    D. keep one hand free so that he can hold on to the railing

Questions 13-18.

DIRECTIONS: Questions 13 through 18 are to be answered SOLELY according to the information given in the following accident report.

DATE: February 2, _____

TO: Edward Moss, Superintendent   SUBJECT: Report of Accident to Philip
     Pacific Houses   Fay, Employee 1825 North
     2487 Shell Road   8th St. Auburnsville, Ill. Iden-
     Auburnsville, Illinois   tification # 374-24

Philip Fay, an employee, came to my office at 10:15 A.M. yesterday and told me that he hurt his left elbow. When I asked him what happened, he told me that 15 minutes ago, while shoveling the snow from in front of Building #14 at 2280 Stone Ave., he slipped on some snow-covered ice and fell on his elbow. Joseph Sanchez and Arthur Campbell, who were working with him, saw what happened.

Mr. Fay complained of pain and could not bend his left arm. I called for an ambulance right away. A police patrol car from the 85th Precinct arrived 15 minutes later, and Patrolman Johnson, Shield #8743, said that an ambulance was on the way. At 10:45 A.M., an ambulance arrived from Auburn Hospital. Dr. Breen examined Mr. Fay and told me that he would have to go to the hospital for some x-ray pictures to determine how bad the injury was. The ambulance left with Mr. Fay at 11:00 A.M.

At 3:45 P.M. Mr. Fay called from the hospital and told me that his arm had been put in a cast in the emergency room of the hospital. He was told that he had fractured his left elbow and would have to stay out of work for about four weeks. He is to report back at the hospital in three weeks for another examination and to see if the cast can be taken off. His wife was at the hospital with him, and they were now going home.

Attached are the statements from the witnesses and our completed *Report of Injury* form.
William Fields
Foreman

13. Which one of the following did NOT see the accident?

    A. Campbell   B. Fay   C. Fields   D. Sanchez

14. The CORRECT date and time of the accident is February _____, A.M.

    A. 2, 10:00   B. 2, 10:15   C. 1, 10:00   D. 1, 10:15

15. The ambulance came about _____ hour after _____.

    A. 1/4; the accident   B. 1/4; it was called
    C. 1/2; the accident   D. 1/2; it was called

16. It is not possible to tell whether Fay went to report the accident right away because the report does NOT say

    A. how long it takes to get from Building #14 to the foreman's office
    B. how long it takes to get from Stone Ave. to Shell Rd.
    C. whether Fay telephoned the foreman first
    D. whether the foreman was in his office as soon as Fay got there

17. From the facts in the report, Fay's action might be criticized because he

    A. did not give the foreman the complete story of what had happened
    B. did not take Campbell or Sanchez with him when he went to the foreman's office in case he should need help on the way
    C. did not remain at the accident site and send Sanchez and Campbell to bring the foreman
    D. telephoned from the hospital and by using his arm to do this he might have aggravated his condition

18. Assuming that the report gives the complete story of this incident, the action of the foreman may be criticized because he did NOT

    A. call an ambulance soon enough
    B. go to the hospital with the ambulance and stay with the injured man until he was discharged
    C. have the injured man sign a release of claim against the department
    D. make an on-the-spot investigation of the accident scene nor take corrective action

19. *He came back to assist his partner.*
    In this sentence, the word *assist* means

    A. call   B. help   C. stop   D. question

20. *A person who is biased cannot be a good foreman.*
    In this sentence, the word *biased* means

    A. easy-going   B. prejudiced
    C. strict   D. uneducated

21. *The lecture for the new employees was brief.*
    In this sentence, the word *brief* means

    A. educational   B. free
    C. interesting   D. short

22. *He was asked to clarify the order.*
    In this sentence, the word *clarify* means

    A. follow out   B. make clear
    C. take back   D. write out

23. *The employee was commended by his foreman.*
    In this sentence, the word *commended* means

    A. assigned   B. blamed   C. picked   D. praised

24. *Before the winter, the lawnmower engine was dismantled.*
    In this sentence, the word *dismantled* means

    A. oiled   B. repaired
    C. stored away   D. taken apart

25. *They excavated a big hole on the project lawn.*
    In this sentence, the word *excavated* means

    A. cleaned out   B. discovered
    C. dug out   D. filled in

26. *The new man was told to sweep the exterior area.*
    In this sentence, the word *exterior* means

    A. asphalt   B. nearby   C. outside   D. whole

27. *He implied that he would work overtime if necessary.*
    In this sentence, the word *implied* means

    A. denied B. explained
    C. guaranteed D. hinted

28. *The bag of the vacuum cleaner was inflated.*
    In this sentence, the word *inflated* means

    A. blown up with air B. filled with dirt
    C. loose D. torn

29. *Burning material during certain hours is prohibited.*
    In this sentence, the word *prohibited* means

    A. allowed B. forbidden C. legal D. required

30. *He was rejected when he applied for the job.*
    In this sentence, the word *rejected* means

    A. discouraged B. put to work
    C. tested D. turned down

31. *The foreman was able to substantiate his need for extra supplies.*
    In this sentence, the word *substantiate* means

    A. estimate B. meet C. prove D. reduce

32. *Sufficient supplies were sent to the housing project.*
    In this sentence, the word *sufficient* means

    A. enough B. maintenance
    C. needed D. new

33. *The new instructions supersede the old ones.*
    In this sentence, the word *supersede* means

    A. explain B. improve C. include D. replace

34. *Shake the broom free of surplus water and hang it up to dry.*
    In this sentence, the word *surplus* means

    A. dirty B. extra C. rinse D. soapy

35. *When a crack is filled, the asphalt must be tamped.*
    In this sentence, the word *tamped* means

    A. cured B. heated
    C. packed down D. wet down

36. *The tenant had a trivial complaint.*
    In this sentence, the word *trivial* means

    A. daily B. housing
    C. serious D. unimportant

37. *The apartment was left vacant.*
    In this sentence, the word *vacant* means

    A. clean B. empty C. furnished D. locked

38. *The caretaker spent the whole day doing various repairs.*
    In this sentence, the word *various* means

    A. different B. necessary C. small D. special

39. When preparing for a mopping operation, fill the standard 16-quart bucket to the 3/4 full mark with warm water. Then add detergent at the rate of 2 oz. per gallon of water and disinfectant at the rate of 1 oz. to 3 gallons of water. According to these directions, the amount of detergent and disinfectant to add to 3/4 of a bucket of warm water is _____ oz. detergent and _____ oz. disinfectant.

    A. 4; 1/2 B. 5; 3/4 C. 6; 1 D. 8; 1 1/4

40. If corn brooms weigh 32 lbs. a dozen, the average weight of one corn broom is CLOSEST to 2 lbs. _____ oz.

    A. 14 B. 11 C. 9 D. 6

41. At the beginning of the year, a foreman has 7 dozen electric bulbs in stock. During the year, he receives a shipment of 14 dozen bulbs, and also replaces 5 burned-out bulbs a month in each of 3 buildings in his area. How many electric bulbs does he have on hand at the end of the year?
    _____ dozen.

    A. 3 B. 6 C. 8 D. 12

42. A project has 4 buildings, each 14 floors high. Each floor has 10 apartments. If 35% of the apartments in the project have 3 rooms or less, how many apartments have 4 or more rooms?

    A. 196 B. 210 C. 364 D. 406

43. An employee takes 1 hour and 30 minutes a day to sweep 30 flights of stairs. How many flights of stairs does he sweep in a month if he spends a total of 30 hours doing this job and works at the same rate?

    A. 200 B. 300 C. 600 D. 900

44. During a month, Employee A washed 30 windows, Employee B washed 4 times as many windows as Employee A, and Employee C washed 1/2 as many windows as Employee B.
    The total number of windows washed by all three men together during this month is

    A. 180 B. 210 C. 240 D. 330

45. How much would it cost to completely fence in the playground area shown at the right with fencing costing $1.50 a foot?
    A. $123.00
    B. $164.00
    C. $177.00
    D. $192.00

    (Diagram shows an L-shaped playground with measurements: 14 FT., 9 FT., 26 FT., 33 FT.)

46. If it takes 2 men 9 days to do a job, how many men are needed to do the same job in 3 days?

    A. 4   B. 5   C. 6   D. 7

47. Suppose that a department operates 1,644 buildings. If one employee is needed for every 2 buildings, and one foreman is needed for every 18 employees, the number of foremen needed is CLOSEST to

    A. 45   B. 50   C. 55   D. 60

48. If 60 bars of soap cost the same as 2 gallons of wax, how many bars of soap can be bought for the price of 5 gallons of wax?

    A. 120 B. 150 C. 180 D. 300

49. An employee waxes 275 sq.ft. of floor on Monday, 352 sq. ft. on Tuesday, 179 sq.ft. on Wednesday, and 302 sq.ft. on Thursday. In order to average 280 sq.ft. of floor waxed a day, how many square feet of floor must he wax on Friday?

    A. 264 B. 278 C. 292 D. 358

50. A project covers 35 acres altogether. Lawns, playgrounds, and walks take up 28 acres and the rest is given over to buildings. What percentage of the total area is given over to buildings?

    A. 7%   B. 20% C. 25% D. 28%

KEY (CORRECT ANSWERS)

1. B	11. B	21. D	31. C	41. B
2. D	12. D	22. B	32. A	42. C
3. B	13. C	23. D	33. D	43. C
4. D	14. C	24. D	34. B	44. B
5. A	15. D	25. C	35. C	45. C
6. C	16. A	26. C	36. D	46. C
7. A	17. B	27. D	37. B	47. A
8. A	18. D	28. A	38. A	48. B
9. C	19. B	29. B	39. C	49. C
10. D	20. B	30. D	40. B	50. B

TEST 3

DIRECTIONS: Each question consists of a statement. You are to indicate whether the statement is TRUE (T) or FALSE (F). *PRINT THE LETTER OF THE CORRECT ANSWER IN THE SPACE AT THE RIGHT.*

1. All injuries and accidents should be reported to your supervisor, even if they are small ones and no one was hurt badly. 1._____

2. If, while working, you find a sealed envelope addressed to a city office, and marked *confidential*, you should first open it up to make sure that there is no money in it, and then turn it over to your supervisor. 2._____

3. If your supervisor asks for your ideas on how to make your work easier, don't give him your suggestions because he will think you're a *wise-guy*. 3._____

4. An important reason for training a city employee on the job is to help him do his work safely and correctly. 4._____

5. When working outdoors during cold weather, you should carry a small bottle of whiskey and take a drink once in a while in order to keep warm. 5._____

6. Male employees of the city are expected to come to work clean-shaven even if they have to work outdoors in all kinds of weather. 6._____

7. You should sign out the time sheet for another man on your job who has left a half-hour early, because he will do the same favor for you some time. 7._____

8. A laborer should never give a member of the public directions to a city office in a building where he works because it is not part of his job and will interfere with his own work. 8._____

9. You should call your supervisor if you can't come to work in the morning so that he can get someone else to take your place for the day if necessary. 9._____

10. A city employee does not have to work as hard as a person working for a private company because civil service employees cannot be fired from their jobs. 10._____

11. *Using the proper tool will aid a worker in doing a better job.*
    In this sentence, the word *aid* means NEARLY the same as *help*. 11._____

12. *The application form has a space for the name of the former employer.*
    In this sentence, the word *former* means NEARLY the same as *new*. 12._____

13. *The exterior of the building needed to be painted.*
    In this sentence, the word *exterior* means NEARLY the same as *inside*. 13._____

14. *The smoke from the fire was dense.*
    In this sentence, the word *dense* means NEARLY the same as *thick*. 14._____

15. *Vacations should be planned in advance.*
    According to this sentence, vacations should be planned ahead of time. 15._____

16. *The employee denied that he would accept another job.*
    In this sentence, the word *denied* means NEARLY the same as *admitted*. 16._____

17. *An annual report is made by the central stockroom.* 17._____
    In this sentence, the word *annual* means NEARLY the same as *monthly*.

18. *Salaries were increased in the new budget.* 18._____
    In this sentence, the word *increased* means NEARLY the same as *cut*.

19. *All excess oil is to be removed from tools.* 19._____
    In this sentence, the word *excess* means NEARLY the same as *extra*.

20. *The new employee did similar work on his last job.* 20._____
    In this sentence, the word *similar* means NEARLY the same as *interesting*.

21. *Helpful employees make favorable impressions on the public.* 21._____
    In this sentence, the word *favorable* means NEARLY the same as *poor*.

Questions 22-27.

DIRECTIONS: Questions 22 through 27 are to be answered SOLELY according to the information given in the following paragraphs.

THE CITY

The City, which at one time in 1789-90 was the capital of the nation, and which was also the capital of the State until 1796, has continued as the financial and economic capital of the United States and has grown to be the greatest city in the country.

The City is great because it has such a large population a total of eight million persons in 1968. This population is larger than the total inhabitants of 41 of 75 of the largest countries in the world. The City requires many homes and buildings to accommodate its residents. The City consists of more than 725,000 buildings, more than half of which are one and two family houses owned by the occupants. More than five hundred hotels, with 128,000 rooms are needed to take care of the visitors to the City; it is estimated that between one and two hundred thousand people visit the City daily.

The harbor is so large that any six of the other leading seaports of the world could be placed in it. Its piers, to accommodate freight and passengers, number 471 and its waterfront covers 770 miles.

22. The City has been the capital of the United States and also the capital of the State. 22._____

23. In 1968, the population of the City was greater than the total population of forty-one of seventy-five of the largest countries in the world. 23._____

24. Over half of all the buildings in the City are one and two family homes which are owned by the people who live in them. 24._____

25. A little under 200,000 people visit the City each year. 25._____

26. The harbor is larger than any other leading seaport. 26._____

27. The harbor is 471 miles long and has 770 piers to take care of passengers and cargo. 27._____

Questions 28-32.

DIRECTIONS: Questions 28 through 32 are to be answered SOLELY according to the information given in the following paragraph.

USING LADDERS

All ladders must be checked each day for any defects before they are used. They should not be used if there are split rails or loose rungs, or if they have become shaky. Two men should handle a step-ladder which is over eight feet in height; one man if the ladder is smaller. One man must face the ladder, and hold it with a firm grasp while the other is working on it. When you climb a ladder, always face it, grasp the siderails, and climb up one rung at a time. You should come down the same way.

28. A ladder which is new does not have to be inspected before it is used.   28.____

29. A ladder with a loose rung may be used if this rung is not stepped on.   29.____

30. A stepladder 6 feet long may be handled by one man.   30.____

31. If a 10 foot stepladder is used, one man must hold the ladder while the other works on it.   31.____

32. The siderails of a ladder do not have to be held when climbing down.   32.____

Questions 33-37.

DIRECTIONS: Questions 33 through 37 are to be answered SOLELY according to the information given in the following paragraph.

TRAFFIC ACCIDENTS

Three auto accidents happened at the corner of Fifth Street and Seventh Avenue. The first, at 7:00 P.M. last night, knocked down a light pole when two cars collided. At 8:15 A.M. this morning, two other autos crashed head on. This afternoon at 12:30 P.M., another pair of cars crashed. One of them jumped the curb, knocked over two traffic signs, and damaged three parked cars at the corner service station. No serious injury to the drivers was reported but all the cars involved were severely damaged.

33. Nine cars were damaged in the three accidents.   33.____

34. The three accidents happened within a period of 14 hours.   34.____

35. A service station is located at the corner of Fifth Street and Seventh Avenue.   35.____

36. In the last accident, both cars jumped the curb and knocked over 2 light poles.   36.____

37. The drivers of the cars in the last accident were badly hurt.   37.____

Questions 38-47.

DIRECTIONS: Questions 38 through 47 are to be answered SOLELY according to the information given in the following paragraphs.

WASHING OF WALLS

The washing of walls is important, since wall-cleaning costs are an expensive item in the operating cost of building maintenance.

There is a right and a wrong way to wash walls. Streaks may be caused by water running down the dry wall below the place where one is working. This can be prevented by first wetting a section of the wall with water; starting at the bottom and working up before starting the actual washing operation with cleaning solution. Then, if the water runs down the wet wall, there will be almost no streaking. While washing a wall, the temperature should be reasonably low, so that the water will not dry on the wall and cause streaks. Once the dirt on the wall is moistened, the wall must be kept wet until the dirt is removed. The washing of walls should be done with good sponges. One sponge should be for cleaning on the dirty wall and one for rinsing.

When working with the cleaning solution, start at the top of the wall and use a circular motion of the sponge and hand. Work across a given section first to the right and then to the left, and so on down to the base.

After the dirt has been removed, take clean, cool water and a clean sponge and go over the wall to be sure that it is perfectly clean and that no traces of the cleaning solution remain on the wall. Even clean water drying unevenly on a wall will cause slight streaks which become noticeable on the walls.

38. The amount of money spent to wash walls is a very small part in the expenses of running a building.   38.____

39. To prevent streaks when washing a wall, an employee should first wet the wall, starting at the top and working down to the base of a wall.   39.____

40. If a wall is wet in the right way, there will be practically no streaks caused by water running down the wet wall.   40.____

41. If the walls are washed when the room is hot, streaks can be caused by water drying too quickly.   41.____

42. Once a dirty wall is made wet with water, it should be dried completely before the dirt is removed.   42.____

43. To wash walls properly, an employee should use at least two good sponges.   43.____

44. When washing with the cleaning solution, start at the bottom of the wall and work to the top, using a circular motion of the hand and sponge.   44.____

45. When washing with the cleaning solution, the correct method is to work across each part of the wall going first to the left and ending on the right.   45.____

46. After the wall has been washed with the cleaning solution, it must be gone over again with clean water to remove any solution which is left on the wall.   46.____

47. When clean water is used to wash a wall, streaks will never appear, even if the wall dries unevenly.   47.____

Questions 48-52.

DIRECTIONS: Questions 48 through 52 are to be answered SOLELY according to the information given in the following paragraph.

LIFTING

Improper lifting of heavy objects is a frequent cause of strains and ruptures. When a heavy object is to be lifted, an employee should stand close to the object and face it squarely. The feet are spread slightly apart and one foot is a little ahead of the other. Then, bend the knees to bring the body down to the object and keep your back comfortably vertical. Raise the object slightly to see if you can lift it alone. If you can, get a firm grasp with both hands, balance the object and raise it by straightening the legs, but still keeping the back erect. The raising motion is gradual, not swift. In this way, you use the leg muscles which are the strongest muscles in the body. This method of lifting prevents strain to the back muscles which are weak and not built for lifting purposes.

48. Many ruptures are the result of not lifting heavy objects in the correct manner.   48.____

49. When an employee lifts a heavy package, he should keep his feet close together in order to balance the load.   49.____

50. When lifting a heavy object, the back should not be bent but kept upright.   50.____

51. It is best to lift heavy objects quickly in order to prevent strains and ruptures.   51.____

52. For purposes of lifting, the leg muscles are stronger than the arm muscles.   52.____

53. If 15 gallons of gasoline cost $4.95, and you use up 10 gallons, then the value of the gasoline which is still left is $1.65.   53.____

54. If it costs $8,400 to pave a street and the State paid 3 times as much as the City, then the City paid $2,800.   54.____

55. If the charge for a long distance telephone call is 50¢ for the first 5 minutes and 7¢ for each minute after that, then for 85¢ a person could speak for 10 minutes.   55.____

56. A full barrel holds 50 gallons of oil, and you take out 6 gallons a day for 5 days, then at the end of this time there would be 15 gallons of oil left in the barrel.   56.____

57. To surround a field 170 feet long by 120 feet wide with fencing costing $2.00 a foot would cost $580.   57.____

58. If 2 feet of chain cost 17¢, then 6 yards of this chain would cost $1.53.   58.____

59. If a group of workmen planted 28 plants on Monday, 33 on Tuesday, 31 on Wednesday, 35 on Thursday, and 28 on Friday, they planted an average of 31 plants a day.   59.____

60. A floor measuring 12 feet by 9 feet contains 36 sq. ft.   60.____

Questions 61-70.

DIRECTIONS: Questions 61 through 70 are to be answered SOLELY according to the information given in the table below.

EMPLOYMENT RECORD

Name of Employee	Type of Employment	Age	Years In City Service	Building Assigned To	No. of Days Vacation Balance	Days Absent Sick
Allen	Permanent	20	2	D	4	10
Bell	Temporary	34	3	A	18	4
Evans	Temporary	20	4	D	10	1
Gold	Permanent	33	10	D	15	7
Hood	Permanent	40	9	B	20	0
King	Permanent	39	20	C	8	2
Lane	Temporary	27	2	B	5	4
Murphy	Permanent	28	7	B	7	6
Owens	Temporary	30	3	A	15	3
Rose	Temporary	22	1	C	0	0
Silver	Permanent	35	14	B	6	12
Thomas	Permanent	24	3	A	14	1
Vale	Permanent	27	5	A	12	9
Williams	Permanent	35	15	B	2	2
Young	Temporary	32	2	D	6	8

61. Most of the employees have been in city service at least 5 years. 61.____

62. There are more permanent employees assigned to Building B than there are temporary employees assigned to Buildings C and D together. 62.____

63. The youngest temporary employee is Rose. 63.____

64. All the employees who have a vacation balance over 12 days are permanent employees. 64.____

65. Allen and Thomas are the only 2 permanent employees who have been in city service less than 4 years. 65.____

66. The employee with the longest and the employee with the shortest period of city service are both assigned to Building C. 66.____

67. Of the employees who are 34 years of age or over, the one with the least years of city service is Hood. 67.____

68. Hood has as much vacation balance as all the other employees together who are assigned to his building. 68.____

69. Buildings A, C, and D have a total of 10 employees, of whom 5 are permanent and 5 are temporary. 69.____

70. Owens has more years in city service and more vacation time than Bell. 70.____

KEY (CORRECT ANSWERS)

1.	T	16.	F	31.	T	46.	T	61.	F
2.	F	17.	F	32.	F	47.	F	62.	T
3.	F	18.	F	33.	T	48.	T	63.	F
4.	T	19.	T	34.	F	49.	F	64.	F
5.	F	20.	F	35.	T	50.	T	65.	T
6.	T	21.	F	36.	F	51.	F	66.	T
7.	F	22.	T	37.	F	52.	T	67.	F
8.	F	23.	T	38.	F	53.	T	68.	T
9.	T	24.	T	39.	F	54.	F	69.	T
10.	F	25.	F	40.	T	55.	T	70.	F
11.	T	26.	T	41.	T	56.	F		
12.	F	27.	F	42.	F	57.	F		
13.	F	28.	F	43.	T	58.	T		
14.	T	29.	F	44.	F	59.	T		
15.	T	30.	T	45.	F	60.	F		

EXAMINATION SECTION
TEST 1

DIRECTIONS: Each question or incomplete statement is followed by several suggested answers or completions. Select the one that BEST answers the question or completes the statement. *PRINT THE LETTER OF THE CORRECT ANSWER IN THE SPACE AT THE RIGHT.*

1. A foreman who <u>expedites</u> a job

   A. abolishes it
   B. makes it bigger
   C. slows it down
   D. speeds it up

2. If a man is working at a <u>uniform</u> speed, it means he is working at a speed which is

   A. changing
   B. fast
   C. slow
   D. steady

3. To say that a caretaker is <u>obstinate</u> means that he is

   A. cooperative
   B. patient
   C. stubborn
   D. willing

4. To say that a caretaker is <u>negligent</u> means that he is

   A. careless
   B. neat
   C. nervous
   D. late

5. To say that something is <u>absurd</u> means that it is

   A. definite
   B. not clear
   C. ridiculous
   D. unfair

6. To say that a foreman is <u>impartial</u> means that he is

   A. fair
   B. improving
   C. in a hurry
   D. watchful

7. A foreman who is <u>lenient</u> is one who is

   A. careless
   B. harsh
   C. inexperienced
   D. mild

8. A foreman who is <u>punctual</u> is one who is

   A. able
   B. polite
   C. prompt
   D. sincere

9. If you think one of your men is too <u>awkward</u> to do a job, it means you think he is too

   A. clumsy
   B. lazy
   C. old
   D. weak

10. A man who is <u>seldom</u> late, is late

    A. always
    B. never
    C. often
    D. rarely

49

11. In lifting a heavy can, a caretaker should keep his

    A. back and knees straight
    B. back bent and knees straight
    C. knees and back bent
    D. knees bent and back straight

12. If a man is injured on the job and it is *likely* that he has broken bones, the foreman should

    A. call for an ambulance
    B. call the superintendent
    C. take him to the hospital in his car
    D. tell the injured man to go to the hospital immediately

13. The MAIN reason for not letting dust cloths or oily rags pile up in storage closets is that

    A. a fire may start from this material
    B. the closet will not look neat and orderly
    C. the oil may soak into the floor and stain it
    D. they take up valuable space which may be put to better uses

14. Suppose, in making your rounds, you come upon a small oil and grease fire in a basement. After putting in a fire alarm, you find the fire extinguisher is out of order. The BEST thing for you to do is to

    A. do nothing since you have put in an alarm
    B. open all the doors and windows
    C. throw earth and sand on the fire
    D. throw water on the fire

15. The BEST thing to do for a man who feels he is about to faint is to

    A. apply a cold compress to his forehead
    B. give him some cold water to drink
    C. lower his head between his knees
    D. move him out to the fresh air

16. In removing the end of a broken bulb from a socket, the caretaker should stick a hard rubber wedge into the socket and

    A. pull the wedge down
    B. push the wedge up
    C. turn the wedge to the right
    D. turn the wedge to the left

17. At the end of the day, all ash is raked from the incinerator firebox. This is done *mainly* to

    A. get it ready for re-use
    B. leave the firebox ready for firing the next day
    C. prevent the fire from relighting itself
    D. put the ash in cans for removal by the Sanitation Department

18. Black smoke from the furnace will indicate 18.____

    A. a lack of draft
    B. that the incinerator fire door is closed
    C. that the incinerator fire door is open
    D. too much draft

19. The time for burning materials in incinerators is limited to the hours between 19.____

    A. 7 a.m. and 4 p.m.   B. 8 a.m. and 6 p.m.
    C. 5 p.m. and 7 a.m.   D. 6 p.m. and 8 a.m.

20. The BEST way to remove chewing gum from the floor is with a 20.____

    A. cloth wet with acid   B. bristle brush
    C. putty knife   D. rubber sponge

21. The 16-inch hair broom is BEST used on 21.____

    A. basement areas   B. cement walks
    C. stair risers   D. stair halls

22. It is MOST important that the slot in the floor saddle of the elevator be kept free of dirt since, otherwise, 22.____

    A. a fire may start   B. it will be unsightly
    C. someone may slip   D. the door will not close

23. Wall panels in elevators should be cleaned with a cloth dipped in 23.____

    A. ammonia in water   B. gasoline
    C. hot water   D. neutral soap solution

24. Before lighting-off the incinerator, material such as rubber should be removed because it 24.____

    A. can be used in cleaning work
    B. may cause a lot of smoke
    C. may clog the incinerator
    D. will not burn well

25. Of the following, the one that would be dangerous to burn in an incinerator is 25.____

    A. camphor balls   B. empty fruit cans
    C. glass   D. paper

KEY (CORRECT ANSWERS)

1. D
2. D
3. C
4. A
5. C

6. A
7. D
8. C
9. A
10. D

11. D
12. A
13. A
14. C
15. C

16. D
17. C
18. A
19. A
20. C

21. D
22. D
23. A
24. B
25. A

———

TEST 2

DIRECTIONS: Each question or incomplete statement is followed by several suggested answers or completions. Select the one that BEST answers the question or completes the statement. *PRINT THE LETTER OF THE COREECT ANSWER IN THE SPACE AT THE RIGHT.*

1. Before the incinerator is lit, it is BEST that the fire door be _____ with the peephole _____.

   A. closed, closed
   B. closed, open
   C. open, closed
   D. open, open

2. A spark arrestor in the incinerator is located

   A. at the top of the flue
   B. between the fire door and the ash door
   C. in the refractory chamber
   D. on the second floor hopper

3. Elevator cleaning is BEST done between

   A. 8 a.m. and 9 a.m.
   B. 9 a.m. and 10 a.m.
   C. 12 noon and 1 p.m.
   D. 2:30 p.m. and 3:30 p.m.

4. The wax solution that is put on floors of elevators once a week is made of _____ part(s) wax and _____ part(s) water.

   A. 1, 1   B. 1, 2   C. 2, 1   D. 3, 2

5. The cleaning of an elevator cab should take *approximately*

   A. 15 minutes
   B. 40 minutes
   C. one hour for every 225 square feet
   D. one hour for every 300 square feet

6. In washing windows, the blade of the squeegee should always be

   A. dried after each stroke
   B. held straight against the glass
   C. used with as much water as possible
   D. wet after each stroke

7. Caretakers are instructed to leave a 4-inch space between the material in an incinerator can and the top of the can. This is done *mainly* to

   A. follow Sanitation Department rules
   B. make it possible to pile cans on top of each other
   C. make the can easier to lift
   D. prevent spilling over of the material

8. A new corn broom should be soaked overnight before using it for the first time. This is done to

   A. help the broom to keep its shape
   B. make it possible to use the broom for scrubbing
   C. make the broom to wear evenly
   D. remove the brittleness of the broom's straws

9. After each day's use of the mop tank, the

   A. compartments and wringer should be rinsed and wiped dry
   B. compartments should be half-filled with clean water
   C. mop wringer should be left in the unreleased position
   D. wheels-should-be oiled and the excess oil wiped off

10. Elevator cab walls should be cleaned with a solution of water and

    A. ammonia
    C. kerosene
    B. carbon tetrachloride
    D. oil

11. A caretaker received $700.00 for having worked from Monday through Friday, 9 a.m. to 5 p.m. with one hour a day for lunch. The number of hours the caretaker would have to work to earn $120.00 is

    A. 10
    C. 700 divided by 120
    B. 6
    D. 700 minus 120

12. If the cost of a broom went up from $4.00 to $6.00, the per cent INCREASE in the original cost is

    A. 20   B. 25   C. 33 1/3   D. 50

13. The *average* of the numbers 3, 5, 7, 8, 12 is

    A. 5   B. 6   C. 7   D. 8

14. The cost of 100 bags of cotton cleaning cloths, 89 pounds per bag, at 7 cents per pound, is

    A. $549.35   B. $623.00   C. $700.00   D. $890.00

15. If 5 1/2 bags of sweeping compound cost $55.00, then 6 1/2 bags would cost

    A. $60.00   B. $62.50   C. $65.00   D. $67.00

16. The cost of cleaning supplies in a project averaged $330.00 a month during the first 8 months of the year. How much can be spent each month for the last four months if the total amount that can be spent for cleaning supplies for the year is $3,880?

    A. $124.00   B. $220.00   C. $310.00   D. $330.00

17. A shelf in a supply closet can safely hold only 100 pounds. A package of paper towels weighs 2 pounds, a carton of disinfectant weighs 8 pounds, and a box of soap weighs 1 pound. There are already 6 cartons of disinfectant and 6 boxes of soap on the shelf. How many packages of towels can be *safely* placed there?

    A. 20   B. 23   C. 25   D. 27

18. A cleaning solution is made up of 4 gallons of water, 1 pint of liquid soap, and 1 pint of ammonia. How many gallons of water is needed to use up a gallon of ammonia?   18.____

    A. 8   B. 16   C. 24   D. 32

19. Suppose a caretaker has 50 stair halls to clean. If he cleans 74% of them, the number of stair halls still UNCLEANED is   19.____

    A. 38   B. 26   C. 24   D. 13

20. If a man has a 12 foot piece of wood and wishes to cut it into two pieces so that one piece is twice as long as the other, the LONGER piece should be _____ feet.   20.____

    A. 7   B. 7 1/2   C. 8   D. 8 1/2

KEY (CORRECT ANSWERS)

1.	D	11.	B
2.	A	12.	D
3.	B	13.	C
4.	C	14.	B
5.	A	15.	C
6.	A	16.	C
7.	D	17.	B
8.	D	18.	D
9.	A	19.	D
10.	A	20.	C

EXAMINATION SECTION
TEST 1

DIRECTIONS: Each question or incomplete statement is followed by several suggested answers or completions. Select the one that BEST answers the question or completes the statement. *PRINT THE LETTER OF THE CORRECT ANSWER IN THE SPACE AT THE RIGHT.*

1. Washing soda is used to
   A. eliminate the need for rinse mopping or wiping
   B. make the cleaning compound abrasive
   C. decrease the wetting power of water
   D. increase the wetting power of water

   1.____

2. Varnish or lacquer may be used as a sealer on floors finished with
   A. asphalt tiles   B. linoleum
   C. rubber tiles   D. cork tiles

   2.____

3. A long-handled deck scrub brush is MOST effective when scrubbing
   A. large open areas   B. stair treads
   C. small flat areas   D. long corridors

   3.____

4. The BEST method for preventing the infestation of a building by rats is to
   A. use cats
   B. use rat traps
   C. eliminate rat harborages in the building
   D. use poisoned bait

   4.____

5. The one of the following which is NOT recommended for prolonging the useful life of a hair broom is to
   A. rotate the brush to avoid wear on one side only
   B. wash the brush by using it as a mop once a week
   C. comb the brush weekly
   D. hang the brush in storage to avoid resting on bristles

   5.____

6. A good indication of the quality of the cleaning operation in a building is the
   A. amount of cleaning material used each month
   B. number of cleaners employed
   C. number of complaints of unsanitary conditions received
   D. number of square feet of hall space cleaned daily

   6.____

7. Spontaneous ignition is MOST likely to occur in a
   A. pile of oily rags
   B. vented fuel oil tank
   C. metal file cabinet filled with papers in file folders
   D. covered metal container containing clean rags

   7.____

8. The MOST important reason for oiling wood floors is that
   A. it keeps the dust from rising during the sweeping process
   B. the need for daily sweeping of classroom floors is eliminated
   C. oiled floors present a better appearance than waxed floors
   D. the wood surface will become waterproof and stain-proof

9. After oil has been sprayed on a wood floor, the sprayed should be cleaned before storing it.
   The USUAL cleaning material for this purpose is
   A. ammonia water B. salt
   C. kerosene D. alcohol

10. It is usually desirable to assign the cleaning of an office to one employee only because
    A. the amount of time wasted through talking is decreased
    B. an employee working alone, by himself, is more efficient
    C. there is no question who is responsible for the work done
    D. working alone reduces the rate and severity of accidents

11. Of each dollar spent on the cleaning of public buildings, the amount spent on cleaning supplies is USUALLY not more than _____ cents.
    A. 5 B. 35 C. 55 D. 75

12. Cleansing powders such as Ajax should NOT be used to clean and polish brass MAINLY because
    A. the brass turns a much darker color
    B. such cleaners have no effect on tarnish
    C. the surface of the brass may become scratched
    D. too much fine dust is raised in the polishing process

13. To remove chalk marks on sidewalks and cemented playground areas, the MOST acceptable cleaning method is
    A. using a brush with warm water
    B. using a brush with warm water containing some kerosene
    C. hosing down such areas with water
    D. using a brush with a solution of muriatic acid in water

14. Of the following solutions, the one MOST often used in washing exterior glass is _____ water and a small quantity of _____.
    A. hot; turpentine B. cold; ammonia
    C. cold; glass wax D. warm; soft soap

15. Rust stains in wash basins can BEST be prevented by
    A. applying wax film to the rusty surface
    B. replacing leaking faucet washers
    C. adding rush inhibitor to the domestic cold water storage tank
    D. sandpapering the rusty surfaces

16. Of the following, the one which is likely to be MOST harmful to asphalt tile is 16.____
    A. coffee   B. ketchup   C. salad oil   D. vinegar

17. Of the following, when sweeping a corridor with a floor brush, the cleaner should 17.____
    A. lean on the brush and walk the length of the corridor
    B. give the brush a slight jerk after each stroke to free it of loose dirt
    C. make certain there is no overlap on sweeping strokes
    D. use moderately long pull strokes

18. Time standards for cleaning are of value ONLY if 18.____
    A. a bonus is promised if the time standards are beaten
    B. the cleaners determine the methods and procedures to be used
    C. accompanied by a completely detailed description of the methods to be used
    D. a schematic diagram of the area is made available to the cleaners

19. In using a floor brush in a corridor, a cleaner should be instructed to 19.____
    A. use moderately long pull strokes whenever possible
    B. make certain that there is no overlap on sweeping strokes
    C. give the brush a slight jerk after each stroke to free it from loose dirt
    D. keep the sweeping surface of the brush firmly flat on the floor to obtain maximum coverage

20. Of the following, the BEST procedure in sweeping classroom floors is: 20.____
    A. Open all windows before beginning the sweeping operation
    B. The cleaner should move forward while sweeping
    C. Alternate pull and push strokes should be used
    D. Sweep under desks on both sides of an aisle while moving down the aisle

21. PROPER care of floor brushes includes 21.____
    A. washing brushes daily after each use with warm soap solution
    B. dipping brushes in kerosene periodically to remove dirt
    C. washing with warm soap solution at least once a month
    D. avoiding contact with soap or soda solutions to prevent drying of bristles

22. An ADVANTAGE of vacuum cleaning rather than sweeping a floor with a floor brush is: 22.____
    A. Stationary furniture will not be touched by the cleaning tool
    B. The problem of dust on furniture is reduced
    C. The initial cost of the apparatus is less than the cost of an equivalent number of floor brushes
    D. Daily sweeping of rooms and corridors can be eliminated

23. Sweeping compound for use on rubber tiles, asphalt tile, or sealed wood floors must NOT contain 23.____
    A. sawdust   B. water   C. oil soap   D. floor oil

24. The one of the following cleaning operations for which a custodian is LEAST likely to use vacuum cleaning equipment is
    A. cleaning blackboard erasers
    B. removing dust from blinds or draperies
    C. cleaning toilet room floors
    D. high dusting of classroom walls

25. In mopping the wood floor of a classroom, it is considered BEST practice to
    A. mop as large an area as possible before rinsing
    B. mop across the grain whenever possible
    C. sweep the floor thoroughly before mopping
    D. start mopping in the front of the room nearest the door entrance

KEY (CORRECT ANSWERS)

1.	D		11.	A
2.	D		12.	C
3.	C		13.	A
4.	C		14.	B
5.	B		15.	B
6.	C		16.	C
7.	A		17.	B
8.	A		18.	C
9.	C		19.	C
10.	C		20.	A

21.	C
22.	B
23.	D
24.	C
25.	C

TEST 2

DIRECTIONS: Each question or incomplete statement is followed by several suggested answers or completions. Select the one that BEST answers the question or completes the statement. *PRINT THE LETTER OF THE CORRECT ANSWER IN THE SPACE AT THE RIGHT.*

1. Of the following cleaning jobs to be done by hand, one cleaner should normally take the LONGEST time to finish a 1,000 square foot area when he is
   A. wet mopping a soft floor
   B. washing a marble floor
   C. wet mopping a hard floor
   D. washing restroom tile

   1.____

2. A cleaner takes an average of forty minutes to mop 1,000 square feet of floor. The amount of time this cleaner should take to mop the floor of a rectangular corridor eight feet wide by sixty feet long is, on the average, MOST NEARLY _____ minutes.
   A. 10   B. 20   C. 30   D. 40

   2.____

3. By normal work standards, the time it should take a cleaner to clean ten toilet bowls is MOST NEARLY _____ minutes.
   A. 5   B. 10   C. 25   D. 50

   3.____

4. An auditorium eighty feet by 100 feet must be swept in one hour. If each cleaner takes fifteen minutes to sweep 1,000 square feet of auditorium, the number of cleaners that must be assigned to complete the sweeping in one hour is
   A. 1   B. 2   C. 3   D. 4

   4.____

5. Under normal circumstances, the one of the following daily jobs which it is LEAST important to complete on a day when only half of your cleaners report for work is the
   A. cleaning of toilets
   B. sweeping of corridors
   C. collecting trash
   D. sweeping of stairs

   5.____

6. A material COMMONLY used in detergents is
   A. rock salt
   B. Glauber's salt
   C. trisodium phosphate
   D. monosodium glutamate

   6.____

7. A disinfectant material is one that will
   A. kill germs
   B. dissolve soil and stop odors
   C. give a clean odor and cover a disagreeable odor
   D. prevent soil buildup

   7.____

8. When scrubbing a wooden floor, it is ADVISABLE to
   A. flood the surface with the cleaning solution in order to float the soil out of all crevices
   B. hose off the loosened soil before starting the scrubbing operation

   8.____

C. pick up the used solution as soon as possible
D. mix a mild acid with the cleaning solution in order to clean the surface quickly

9. Before starting a wall washing operation, it is BEST to
   A. check the temperature of the water
   B. soak the sponge to be used
   C. check the pH of the mixed cleaning solution
   D. dust the wall to be washed

10. The device which is LEAST likely to be used by the custodian in cleaning minor stoppages in the plumbing system is a
    A. snake   B. auger   C. plunger   D. trowel

11. The first aid treatment for chemical burns on the skin is
    A. treatment with ointment and then bandaging
    B. washing with large quantities of water and then treating as heat burns
    C. treatment with a neutralizing agent and no bandage
    D. application of sodium bicarbonate and then bandaging

12. The chemical MOST frequently used to clean drains clogged with grease is
    A. muriatic acid   B. soda ash   C. ammonia   D. caustic soda

13. The one of the following terms which BEST describes the size of a water pail is
    A. 10 quart   B. 32 ounce
    C. 24 inch O.D.   D. 10 square feet

14. The one of the following terms which BEST describes the size of a floor scrubber brush is
    A. 10 quart   B. 32 ounce
    C. 24 inch O.D.   D. 10 square feet

15. Of the following items, the one which is BEST to use when dusting a mahogany table is a
    A. feather duster   B. treated cotton cloth
    C. crocus cloth   D. wet sponge

16. The one of the following tasks which should be a two-man assignment is
    A. vacuum cleaning a rug
    B. sweeping a classroom
    C. washing blackboards in a classroom
    D. washing fluorescent light fixtures

17. The BEST way to remove some small pieces of broken glass from a floor is to
    A. use a brush and dustpan
    B. pick up the pieces carefully with your hands
    C. use a wet mop and a wringer
    D. sweep the pieces into the corner of the room

18. There is a two-light fixture in the room where you are working. One of the lightbulbs goes out, and you need more light to work by.
You should
    A. change the fuse in the fuse box
    B. have a new bulb put in
    C. call for an electrician and stop work until he comes
    D. find out what is causing the short circuit

18.____

19. While working on the job, you accidentally break a window pane. No one is around, and you are able to clean up the broken pieces of glass.
It would then be BEST for you to
    A. leave a note near the window that a new glass has to be put in because it was accidentally broken
    B. forget about the whole thing because the window was not broken on purpose
    C. write a report to your supervisor telling him that you saw a broken window pane that has to be fixed
    D. tell your supervisor that you accidentally broke the window pane while working.

19.____

Questions 20-23.

DIRECTIONS: Questions 20 through 23 are to be answered on the basis of the information given in the following passage.

MOPPING FLOORS

When mopping hardened cement floors, either painted or unpainted, a soap and water mixture should be used. This should be made by dissolving half a cup of soft soap in a pail of hot water. It is not desirable, however, under any circumstances, to use a soap and water mixture on cement floors that are not hardened. For mopping this type of floor, it is recommended that the cleaning agent be made up of 2 ounces of laundry soda mixed in a pail of water.

Soaps are not generally used on hard tile floors because slippery films may build up on the floor. It is generally recommended that these floors be mopped using a pail of hot water in which has been mixed 2 ounces of washing powder for each gallon of water. The floors should then be rinsed thoroughly.

After the mopping is finished, proper care should be taken of the mop. This is done by first cleaning the mop in clear warm water. Then it should be wrung out, after which the strands of the mop should be untangled. Finally, the mop should be hung up by its handle to dry.

20. According to the above passage, you should NEVER use a soap and water mixture when mopping _____ floors.
    A. hardened cement   B. painted
    C. unhardened cement   D. unpainted

20.____

21. According to the above passage, using laundry soap mixed in a pail of water as a cleaning agent is recommended for
    A. all floors
    B. all floors except hard tile floors
    C. some cement floors
    D. linoleum floor coverings only

22. According to the above passage, the GENERALLY recommended mixture for mopping hard tile floors is _____ of hot water.
    A. ½ cup of soft soap for each gallon
    B. ½ cup of soft soap in a pail
    C. 2 ounces of washing powder in a pail
    D. 2 ounces of washing powder for each gallon

23. According to the above passage, the PROPER care of a mop after it is used includes
    A. cleaning it in clear cold water and hanging it by its handle to dry
    B. wringing it out, untangling, and drying it
    C. untangling its strands before wringing it out
    D. untangling its strands while cleaning it in clear water

24. The FIRST operation in routine cleaning of toilets and washrooms is to
    A. wash floors
    B. clean walls
    C. clean washbasins
    D. empty waste receptacles

25. To eliminate the cause of odors in toilet rooms, the tile floor should be mopped with
    A. a mild solution of soap and trisodium phosphate in water
    B. dilute lye solution followed by a hot water rinse
    C. dilute muriatic acid dissolved in hot water
    D. carbon tetrachloride dissolved in hot water

KEY (CORRECT ANSWERS)

1. D
2. B
3. C
4. B
5. D

6. C
7. A
8. C
9. D
10. D

11. B
12. D
13. A
14. C
15. B

16. D
17. A
18. B
19. D
20. C

21. C
22. D
23. B
24. D
25. A

TEST 3

DIRECTIONS: Each question or incomplete statement is followed by several suggested answers or completions. Select the one that BEST answers the question or completes the statement. *PRINT THE LETTER OF THE CORRECT ANSWER IN THE SPACE AT THE RIGHT.*

1. The one of the following cleaning agents that should be used to remove an accumulation of grease from a concrete driveway is a(n)
   A. acid cleaner
   B. alkaline cleaner
   C. liquid soap
   D. solvent cleaner

   1._____

2. Of the following, the cleaning assignment which you would LEAST prefer to have performed *during* school hours is
   A. sweeping of corridors and stairs
   B. cleaning and polishing brass fixture
   C. cleaning toilets
   D. dusting of offices, halls, and special rooms

   2._____

3. Specifications concerning window cleaners' anchors and safety belts must be in compliance with the rules and regulations outlined in the
   A. State Labor Law and Board of Standards and Appeals
   B. Building Code
   C. Fire Department Safety Manual
   D. National Protection Association

   3._____

4. The difficulty of cleaning soil from surfaces is LEAST affected by the
   A. length of time between cleanings
   B. chemical nature of the soil
   C. smoothness of the surface being cleaned
   D. standard time allotted to the job

   4._____

5. The one of the following chemicals that a custodian should tell a cleaner to use is to remove mildew from terrazzo is
   A. ammonia
   B. oxalic acid
   C. sodium hypochlorite
   D. sodium silicate

   5._____

6. Of the following, the one which is NOT a purpose of a cleaning job breakdown is to
   A. eliminate unnecessary steps
   B. determine the type of floor wax to use
   C. rearrange the sequence of operations to save time
   D. combine steps or actions where practicable

   6._____

7. The BEST time of day to dust classroom furniture and woodwork is
   A. in the morning before the students arrive
   B. during the morning recess
   C. during the students' lunch time
   D. immediately after the students are dismissed for the day

   7._____

66

2 (#3)

8. In order to clean an office with 20,000 square feet of space in four hours, using a standard of 900 square feet per hour, the number of cleaners you should assign to do the job is MOST NEARLY 8._____
   A. 4 B. 6 C. 8 D. 10

9. The area of a floor 35' wide and 45' long is, in square yards, MOST NEARLY 9._____
   A. 175 B. 262 C. 525 D. 1575

10. One of the important benefits to floors that wax does NOT provide is 10._____
    A. easier soil remover B. improved stain resistance
    C. reduction in wear D. resistance to fire

11. Domestic hot water storage reservoirs should be thoroughly cleaned once 11._____
    A. a week B. a month
    C. a year D. every two years

Questions 12-14.

DIRECTIONS: Questions 12 through 14 are to be answered on the basis of the following passage.

The method of cleaning which should generally be used is the space assignment method. Under this method, the buildings to be cleaned are divided into different sections. Within each section, each crew of cleaners is assigned to do one particular cleaning job. For example, within a section, one crew may be assigned to cleaning offices, another to scrubbing floors, a third to collection trash, and so on. Other methods which may be used are the post assignment method, and the gang cleaning method. Under the post assignment method, a cleaner is assigned to one area of a building and performs all cleaning jobs in that area. This method is seldom used except where buildings are so small and distant from each other that it is not economical to use the space assignment method. Under the gang cleaning method, a custodian takes a number of cleaners through a section of the building. These cleaners work as a group and complete the various cleaning jobs as they go. This method is generally used only where the building contains very large open areas.

12. According to the above passage, under the space assignment method, each crew GENERALLY 12._____
    A. works as a group and does a variety of different cleaning jobs
    B. is assigned to one are and performs all cleaning jobs in that area
    C. does one particular cleaning job within a section of a building
    D. follows the custodian through a building containing large, open areas

13. According to the above passage, the post assignment method is used MOSTLY where the building to be cleaned are _____ in size and situated _____. 13._____
    A. large; close together B. small, close together
    C. large; far apart D. small; far apart

14. As used in the above passage, the word *economical* means MOST NEARLY 14._____
    A. thrifty B. agreed C. unusual D. wasteful

15. New copper flashing that has been soldered should be cleaned with
    A. muriatic acid
    B. plain water
    C. benzene
    D. washing soda or lye

16. To improve the appearance and preserve a rubber tile floor, the BEST substance to use is
    A. wax
    B. floor seal varnish
    C. plastic floor finish
    D. none of the above

17. When waxing asphalt tile floors, the wax should be applied in several thin coats because
    A. one thick coat takes longer to apply
    B. it will dry faster and harder
    C. it is a more economical method
    D. the pores of the tile will be able to absorb the wax more readily

18. The floors of modern indoor swimming pools are USUALLY cleaned of sediment by means of
    A. long-handled wire brushes
    B. vacuum cleaning equipment
    C. water-resistant fiber brushes
    D. compressed air wall brush

19. A good disinfectant is one that will
    A. have a clean odor which will cover up disagreeable odors
    B. destroy germs and create more sanitary condition
    C. dissolve encrusted dirt and other sources of disagreeable odors
    D. dissolve grease and other materials that may cause stoppages in toilet waste lines

20. The surfaces of water coolers and door kick plates are cleaned BEST by using a cleaning solution and a
    A. brush
    B. wet cloth
    C. cellulose sponge
    D. wab of paper

21. When the diaphragm or bellows of a thermostatic radiator trap is found to be dirty. It is USUALLY cleaned with
    A. turpentine
    B. carbon tetrachloride
    C. kerosene
    D. mild soap and water

22. In general, the MOST efficient method for doing a cleaning job is the method which
    A. must be repeated most frequently
    B. has the most different steps and operations
    C. gives the best results for the least amount of effort
    D. requires the efforts of the greatest number of cleaners

23. Chloride of lime should be used for the removal of
    A. alkali stains on wood
    B. grass stains on wood or marble
    C. indelible pencil and marking ink stains on concrete or terrazzo
    D. ink stains on wood

24. The one of the following that is a concrete floor sealer is
    A. sodium silicate	B. neatsfoot oil
    C. sodium hydroxide	D. linseed oil

25. The MAIN reason for applying floor finish to a floor surface is to
    A. protect against germs	B. protect the floor surface
    C. increase traction	D. waterproof the floor

KEY (CORRECT ANSWERS)

1.	D	11.	C
2.	C	12.	C
3.	A	13.	D
4.	D	14.	A
5.	C	15.	D
6.	B	16.	A
7.	A	17.	B
8.	B	18.	B
9.	A	19.	B
10.	D	20.	C

21. C
22. C
23. C
24. A
25. B

MECHANICAL APTITUDE
TOOL RECOGNITION AND USE

EXAMINATION SECTION
TEST 1

DIRECTIONS: Each question or incomplete statement below is followed by several suggested answers or completions. Select the one that *BEST* answers the question or completes the statement.

KEY : CORRECT ANSWERS APPEAR AT THE END OF THIS TEST.

1.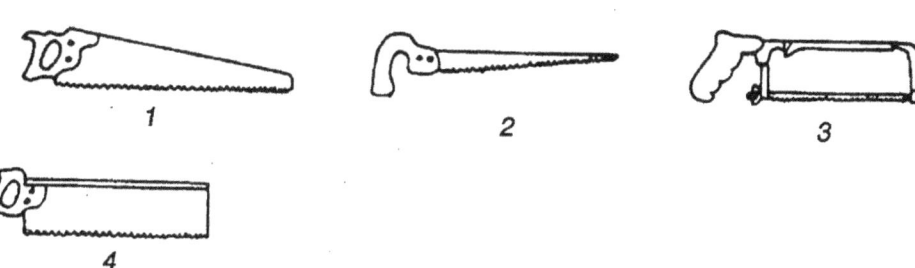

   The saw that is used principally where curved cuts are to be made is numbered

   1. 1   2. 2   3. 3   4. 4

2.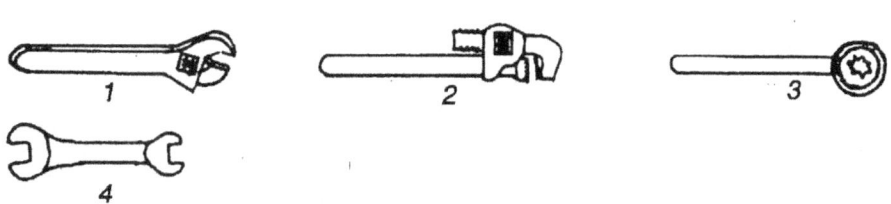

   The wrench that is used principally for pipe work is numbered

   1. 1   2. 2   3. 3   4. 4

3.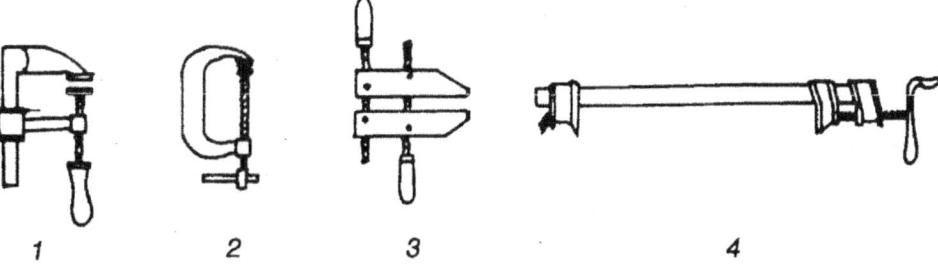

   The carpenter's "hand screw" is numbered

   1. 1   2. 2   3. 3   4. 4

4.

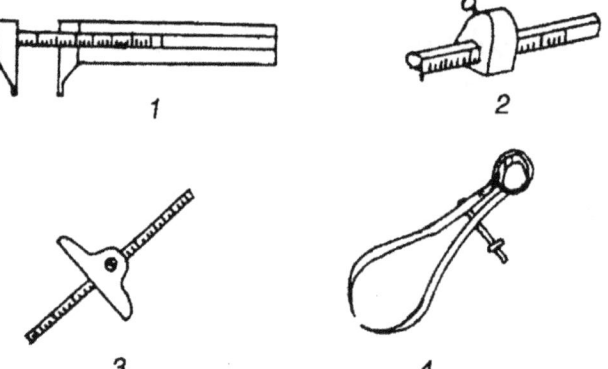

The tool used to measure the depth of a hole is numbered

1. 1   2. 2   3. 3   4. 4

5.

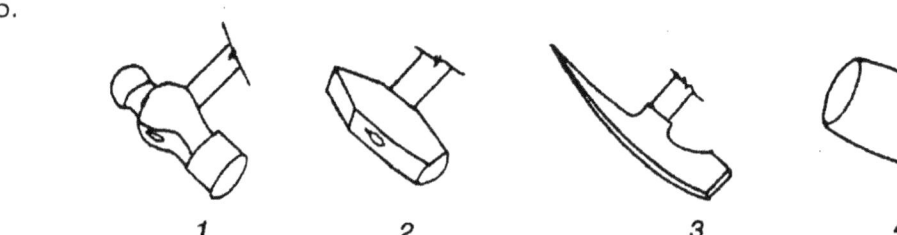

The tool that is best suited for use with a wood chisel is numbered

1. 1   2. 2   3. 3   4. 4

6.

The screw head that would be tightened with an "Allen" wrench is numbered

1. 1   2. 2   3. 3   4. 4

7.

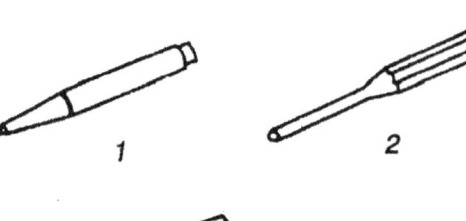 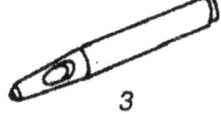

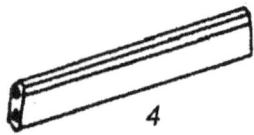

The center punch is numbered

1. 1   2. 2   3. 3   4. 4

3 (#1)

8.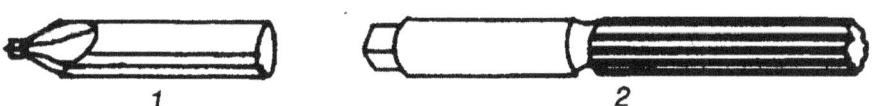

The tool used to drill a hole in concrete is numbered

1. 1 2. 2 3. 3 4. 4

9.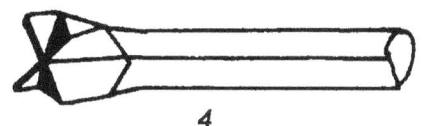

The wrench whose principal purpose is to hold taps for threading is numbered

1. 1 2. 2 3. 3 4. 4

10.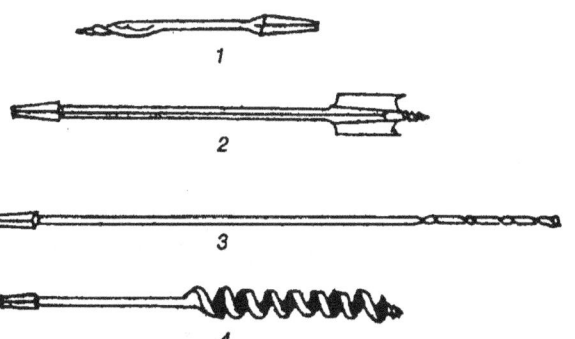

The electrician's bit is indicated by the number

1. 1 2. 2 3. 3 4. 4

73

11. The head of a cold chisel is "mushroomed" as shown in the sketch. 11.____
The use of a chisel in this condition is poor practice because
   1. it is impossible to hit the head squarely
   2. the chisel will not cut accurately
   3. chips might fly from the head
   4. the chisel has lost its "temper"

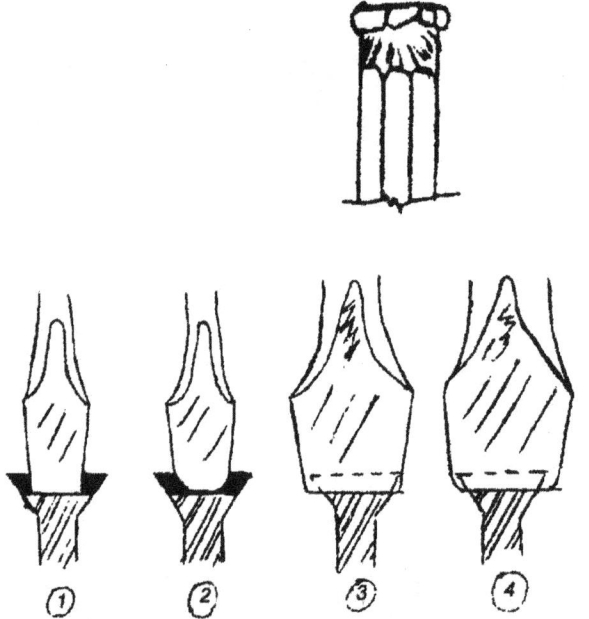

12. The above diagrams show a section of a screw with a screwdriver that is to be used with   12.____
the screw. The one of the diagrams that shows the correct shape of screwdriver is
   1. 1   2. 2   3. 3   4. 4

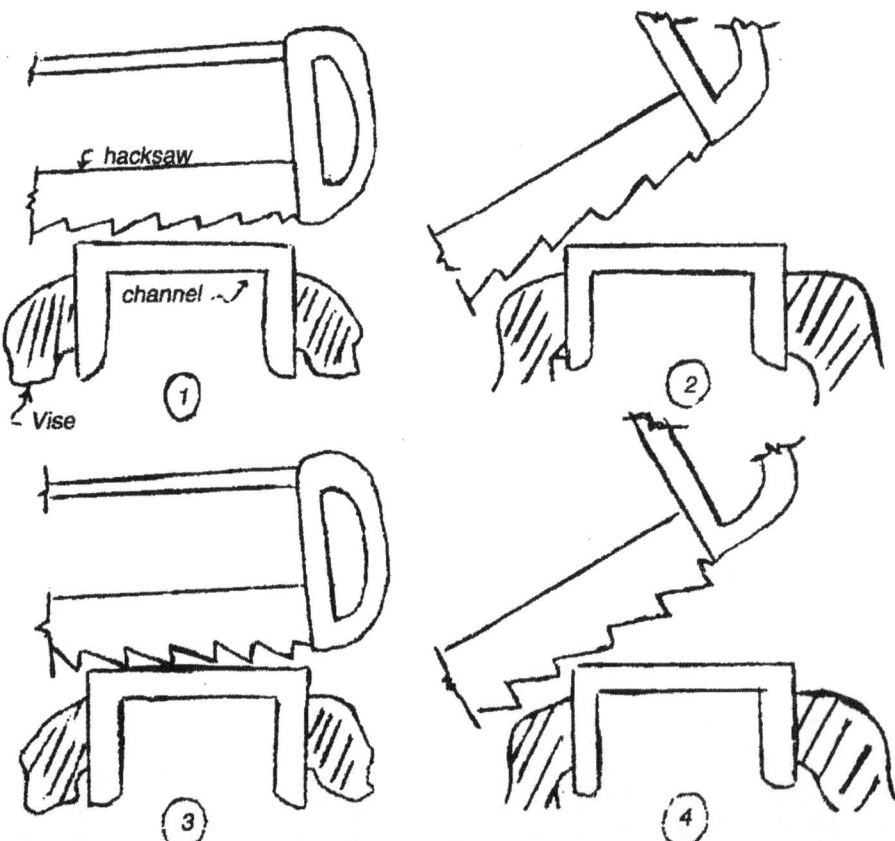

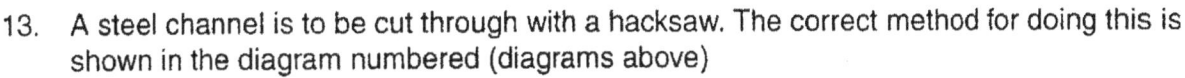

13. A steel channel is to be cut through with a hacksaw. The correct method for doing this is shown in the diagram numbered (diagrams above)   13.____

    1. 1   2. 2   3. 3   4. 4

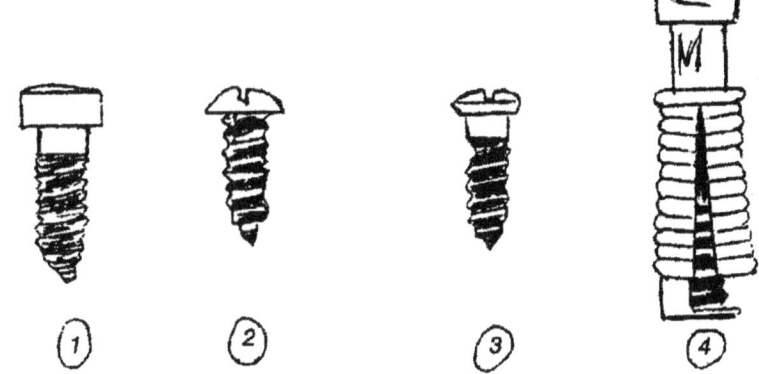

14. The screw above that is most frequently used for sheet metal work is numbered   14.____

    1. 1   2. 2   3. 3   4. 4

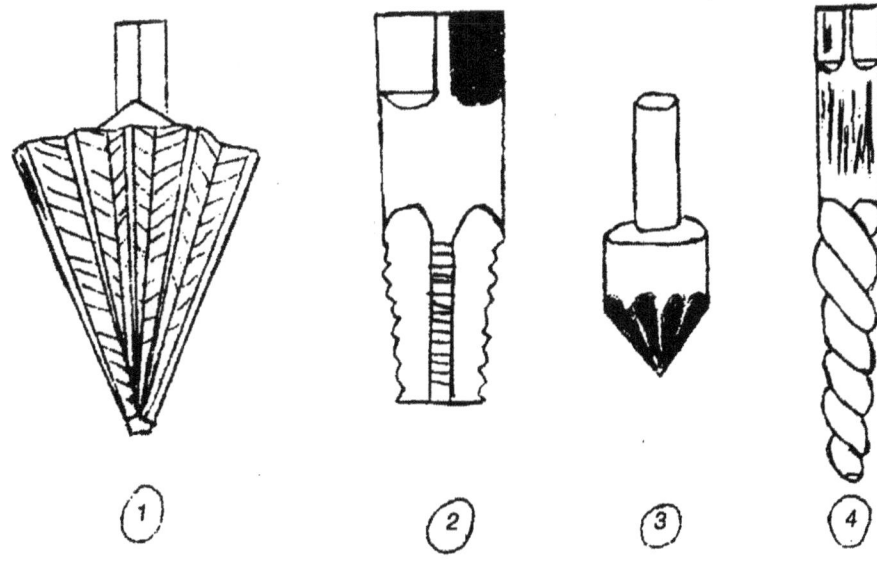

15. The tool used to ream the ends of pipe after the pipe has been cut is shown above in the diagram numbered   15.___

    1. 1 2. 2 3. 3 4. 4

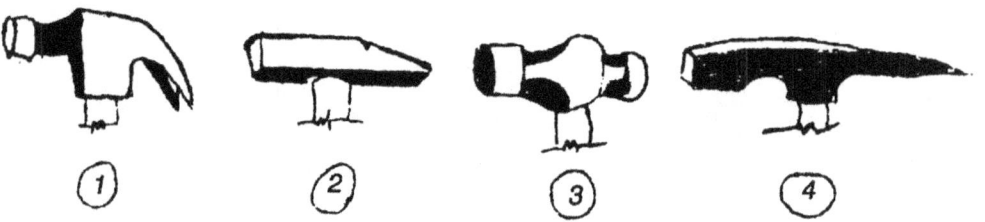

16. The hammer that would be used by a mason to trim brick is shown in the above diagram numbered   16.___

    1. 1 2. 2 3. 3 4. 4

17. The saw intended especially to make accurate miter cuts is shown in the above diagram numbered   17.___

    1. 1 2. 2 3. 3 4. 4

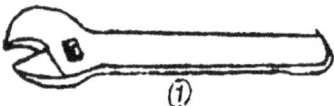 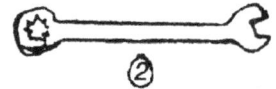

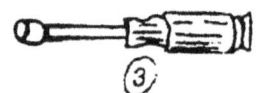 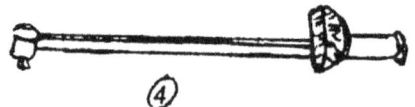

18. A wrench used to tighten cylinder head bolts to a specified torque is shown in the above diagram numbered   18._____

    1. 1   2. 2   3. 3   4. 4

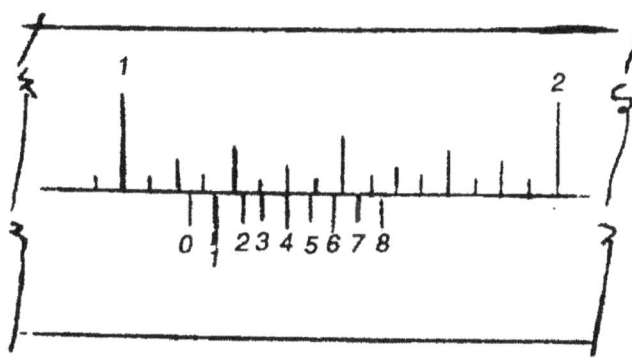

19. A section of the scale of a vernier caliper is shown above. The reading of this caliper setting is most nearly   19._____

    1. 1 3/8   2. 1 5/64   3. 1 5/32   4. 1 7/64

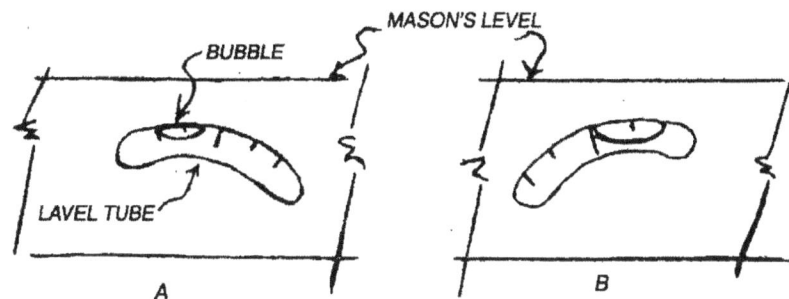

20. A level is placed on a table and the bubble moves to the position indicated in diagram A above. The level is then turned end for end and placed in the same location on the table as before. The bubble now appears as shown in diagram B. The one of the following statements that is correct is   20._____

    1. the left end of the table is higher than the right end
    2. the right end of the table is higher than the left end
    3. it is impossible to tell which end of the table is higher
    4. the level tube is not set properly in the level

21. The flat-head screw is No.   21._____

    1. 1   2. 2   3. 3   4. 4

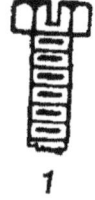 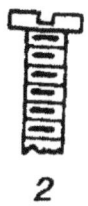 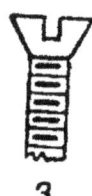 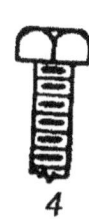

22. The "Phillips" head is No. 22.___

  1. 1   2. 2   3. 3   4. 4

 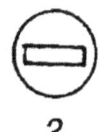  

23. The standard coupling for rigid electrical conduit is 23.___

  1. 1   2. 2   3. 3   4. 4

  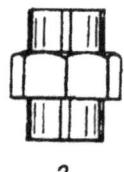 

24. The shape of nut most commonly used on electrical terminals is 24.___

  1. 1   2. 2   3. 3   4. 4

25. The stove bolt is 25.___

  1. 1   2. 2   3. 3   4. 4

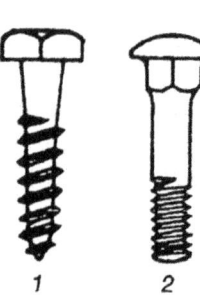   

KEY (CORRECT ANSWERS)

1.	2	11.	3
2.	2	12.	1
3.	3	13.	1
4.	3	14.	2
5.	4	15.	1
6.	3	16.	4
7.	1	17.	3
8.	4	18.	4
9.	1	19.	3
10.	3	20.	4

21. 3
22. 4
23. 1
24. 2
25. 3

EXAMINATION SECTION

TEST 1

DIRECTIONS: Each question or incomplete statement is followed by several suggested answers or completions. Select the one that BEST answers the question or completes the statement. *PRINT THE LETTER OF THE CORRECT ANSWER IN THE SPACE AT THE RIGHT.*

Questions 1-7.

DIRECTIONS: Questions 1 through 7 are to be answered SOLELY on the basis of the information given in the paragraph below and the Visitor's Release form.

On Friday, December 19, at 9:15 A.M., Joan Sanford, who represented the Adam Hart Manufacturing Company, appeared at the Property Protection Agent booth at the 207th Street, Manhattan, Main Shop. She stated that she wanted to see Superintendent Patterson about a parts contract with her firm, which makes spare parts for subway cars. The Agent called Mr. Patterson, who said he expected her. The Agent thereupon asked her to complete a Visitor's Release form, which she did. O the form she indicated her age as 27, her occupation as salesperson, her supervisor's name as Lawrence Austin, the firm's location at 1427 Cedar St., Glendale, N.Y., and her home address as 25-16 65th Road, Oak Point, N.Y. Agent Paul Jones signed the Visitor's Release form as witness to her signature. She then entered the facility and left Transit Authority property at 2 P.M., at which time Mr. Jones gave Miss Sanford a copy of the Visitor's Release form.

TRANSIT AUTHORITY
<u>VISITOR'S RELEASE</u>

The undersigned hereby agrees to hold harmless and indemnify The City of New York, Metropolitan Transportation Authority, New York City Transit Authority, and their respective members, officers, agents, and employees, from any and all loss and liability for damages on account of injuries (including death) to persons and damage to property attributable in whole or in part to the negligence of the undersigned while on or about the premises of the New York City Transit Authority.

```
NYCTA Location to be Visited:_____(1)_____
Duration of Visit: From _____A.M. _____P.M. _____
                   To   _____A.M. _____P.M. _____(2)
Reason for Visit:_____(3)_____
Age: (4)    Occupation: _____(5)_____
Firm Represented:_____(6)_____
Employer: _____(7)_____
Address of Firm: _____(8)_____
Dated:   (9)    (Signed)_____(10)_____
         Address:_____(11)_____
Witness: _____(12)_____
```

1. Which of the following should be on Line 4? 1.____
   A. 2 P.M.
   B. 57
   C. 107th St. Shop
   D. 27

2. Which of the following should be on Line 6? 2.____
   A. Joan Sanford
   B. Adam Hart Manufacturing Co.
   C. Oak Point Associates
   D. Patterson Manufacturing Co.

3. Which of the following should be on Line 11? 3.____
   A. 1427 Cedar St., Glendale, N.Y.
   B. 25-16 65th Road, Oak Point, N.Y.
   C. 3961 Tenth Avenue, Manhattan, at 207th St.
   D. 26-15 65th Ave., Oak Point, N.Y.

4. Which of the following should be on Line 12? 4.____
   A. Miss Sanford's signature
   B. Mr. Patterson's signature
   C. Paul Jones' signature
   D. Lawrence Austin's name

5. On which of the following lines should *1327 Cedar St., Glendale, N.Y.* be entered? 5.____
   A. 2   B. 3   C. 7   D. 8

6. What is Miss Sanford's occupation? 6.____
   A. Superintendent
   B. Protection Agent
   C. Salesperson
   D. Manager, Sales

7. Which of the following should be entered in Section 2 of the form? 7.____
   A. 9:00; 2:00   B. 9:15; 2:00   C. 9:15; 2:15   D. 9:15; 3:00

Questions 8-17.

DIRECTIONS: Questions 8 through 17 are to be answered SOLELY on the basis of the following paragraphs titled SCRAP TRANSFER and the Record of Scrap Award Form.

Protection Agent Robert Green, Pass No. 104123, was assigned to Post 27A at the main entrance of the Fifth Ave. Brooklyn Train Yard on Thursday, October 23 on the 8 A.M.-to-4 P.M. tour. At 10:10 A.M., a scrap removal truck, No. 64, license plate AB-4126, from the J.H. Trucking Company stopped at the gate. The driver showed Agent Green a scrap contract with Award No. 1626 for the removal of 12 headlamps from this location.

Agent Green called Supervisor Raymond Hadley in Storeroom 18 for verification of the award. Supervisor Hadley verified the award. The driver then proceeded to Storeroom 18, where he loaded the headlamps into the truck. Hadley then made out a Materials Permit, signed it, and placed his pass number (521800) on it, and gave it to the driver. At the gate, the driver presented the Materials Permit to Agent Green, who logged out the truck at 10:40 A.M., whereupon the truck left for its destination in the Bronx.

3 (#1)

Agent Green transcribed the information on his registry sheet and the Materials Permit to a Record of Scrap Award form, which he handed to Line Supervisor Brian Sullivan (Pass No. 756349), who had just arrived at the post. Line Supervisor Sullivan, after having checked the form carefully, signed it and wrote his pass number on it.

RECORD OF SCRAP AWARD

Date _____(1)_____
Post No. _____(2)_____   Tour _____(3)_____
Name of Carrier _____(4)_____   Award No. _____(5)_____
Truck License No. _____(6)_____
Truck No. _____(7)_____
Destination: _____
Time In: _____(9)_____   Time Out: _____(10)_____
Description of Scrap: _____(11)_____
Amount: _____(12)_____
Name of Supervisor or Designee: _____(13)_____
Pass No. _____

_____(14)_____   _____(15)_____
TRANSIT PROPERTY PROTECTION AGENT   PASS NO.

_____(16)_____   _____(17)_____
LINE SUPERVISOR SIGNATURE   PASS NO.

8. Which of the following should be on Line 2?
   A. 27A
   B. Coney Island
   C. Storeroom 18
   D. Main Gate

9. Which of the following should be on Line 3?
   A. 12 Midnight – 8 A.M.
   B. 12 P.M. – 8 P.M.
   C. 8 A.M. – 4 P.M.
   D. 4 P.M. – 12 P.M.

10. Which of the following should be on Line 4?
    A. J.H. Trucking Co.
    B. Line Supervisor Sullivan
    C. Transit Authority
    D. Storeroom 18

11. Which of the following should be on Line 8?
    A. Fifth Ave. Yard
    B. Bronx, N.Y.
    C. Storeroom 18
    D. Post 27A

12. Which of the following should be on Line 10?
    A. 9:10 A.M.   B. 10:10 A.M.   C. 10:30 A.M.   D. 10:40 A.M.

13. Which of the following should be on Line 16? _____ signature.
    A. Robert Green's
    B. Brian Sullivan's
    C. the truck driver's
    D. Raymond Hadley's

14. On which of the following lines should *104123* be entered? 14.____
    A. 10   B. 12   C. 15   D. 17

15. On which of the following lines should *AB4216* be entered? 15.____
    A. 1   B. 3   C. 6   D. 13

16. On which of the following lines should *12 headlamps* be entered? 16.____
    A. 3   B. 11   C. 14   D. 17

17. On which of the following lines should *10:10 A.M.* be entered? 17.____
    A. 8   B. 9   C. 10   D. 11

Questions 18-22.

DIRECTIONS: Questions 18 through 22 are to be answered SOLELY on the basis of the information in the KEY STATIONS DIRECTORY below. Key Stations are locations which Protection Agents must visit and inspect on their hourly rounds.

KEY STATIONS DIRECTORY

Key Station No.
1	Protection Agent's booth at Flushing Train Yard
2	On parking lot fence adjacent to No. 4 track
3	On stairwell No. 8 in the Boiler Room
4	On the door leading to the second floor men's locker room
5	Alongside the soda machine in the second floor lunchroom
6	On the oilhouse door
7	Alongside the bulletin board in the main shop
8	Next to fire extinguisher No. 12 on the wall to the left of the entrance to the Supervisor's Office
9	On the bumper block of Track No. 10

18. The number of the key station near the main shop bulletin board is 18.____
    A. 5   B. 6   C. 7   D. 8

19. Where is Key Station No. 4? 19.____
    A. On the parking lot fence adjacent to Track 4
    B. On the door of the second floor men's locker room
    C. On the oilhouse door
    D. In the second floor lunchroom

20. The number of the key station in the Protection Agent's booth is 20.____
    A. 1   B. 3   C. 7   D. 9

21. No. 5 key station is located 21.____
    A. next to fire extinguisher No. 6 in the Protection Agent's booth
    B. on the bumper block of Track 10
    C. in the second floor lunchroom next to the soda machine
    D. on the parking lot fence near Track No. 4

22. The number of the key station on the parking lot fence adjacent to Track No. 4 is

    A. 1 B. 2 C. 3 D. 8

22.____

Questions 23-25.

DIRECTIONS: Questions 23 through 25 are to be answered SOLELY on the basis of the information contained in the following instructions on FIRST AID KITS.

FIRST AID KITS

First aid kits will be used only in case of injury to employees or passengers. A <u>Report of Use of First Aid Kit</u> form will be prepared in triplicate and forwarded to the Station Department Office whenever the seal of the kit is broken, regardless of whether any of the contents is used.

After use, the kit will be temporarily resealed with a shurlock seal bearing the impress of the booth punch. An outside tag will be attached to the seal with the following information on the back of the tag.

```
Opened:_____A.M./P.M.        _____
         (Time)                        (Date)
By:_____
      (Name)              (Title)           (Pass No.)
Resealed:_____A.M./P.M. _____
         (Time)                        (Date)
By:_____
      (Name)              (Title)           (Pass No.)
```

Upon receipt of <u>Report of use of First Aid Kit</u> form, the P.M. Station Supervisor will arrange to replace the items used and reseal the kit, using a special seal pouch.

23. First aid kits may be used whenever
    A. the seal of the kit is broken
    B. the Station Supervisor approves
    C. their contents have to be checked
    D. there is an injury to employees or passengers

23.____

24. Who should arrange for the replacement of the items used in a first aid kit?
    A. Station Agent   B. Cleaner
    C. Station Supervisor   D. Employee who used the kit

24.____

25. The information written on the back of the tag attached to the first aid kit should contain the
    A. social security number of the person who opened the kit
    B. pass number of the person who resealed the kit
    C. time when the accident took place
    D. place where the accident happened

25.____

KEY (CORRECT ANSWERS)

1.	D	11.	B/C
2.	B	12.	D
3.	B	13.	B
4.	C	14.	C
5.	D	15.	C
6.	C	16.	B
7.	B	17.	B
8.	A	18.	C
9.	C	19.	B
10.	A	20.	A

21.	C
22.	B
23.	D
24.	C
25.	B

TEST 2

DIRECTIONS: Each question or incomplete statement is followed by several suggested answers or completions. Select the one that BEST answers the question or completes the statement. *PRINT THE LETTER OF THE CORRECT ANSWER IN THE SPACE AT THE RIGHT.*

Questions 1-6.

DIRECTIONS: Questions 1 through 6 are to be answered SOLELY on the basis of the information contained in the CLEANING REPORT BELOW.

CLEANING REPORT

To: Cleaner (TA) <u>J. Brown</u>, Badge No. <u>3461</u>, Pass No. <u>327351</u>

The following cleaning report must be filled out by you and handed in before you go off duty. Part I shall be prepared by a Station Supervisor, Assistant Station Supervisor, Railroad Clerk, or Claim Investigator. Part II must then be filled out by you.

PART I
This part must be filled in by Station Supervisor, Assistant Station Supervisor, Railroad Clerk, or Claim Investigator before second part is completed by Cleaner (TA).

Date of Accident: *Feb. 17*, Time: *11:20* A.M./P.M. Line: *(A)*, Station: *34th Street*, Exact Location: *Stairway S-6* Name of Injured: *Gregory Peckham* Address: *124 W. 16th St., N.Y.,N.Y.* Accident occurred before/while/after *John Brown* Title: *Cleaner (TA)* Pass No.: *327751* came on duty/was on duty/went off duty.

PART II
This part must be completed and all questions answered by the above Cleaner but only after Part I has been filled in. I *John Brown*, Pass No. *327751* was on duty at the *34th St.* Station on *Feb. 27* from *8:00* A.M./P.M. to *4:00* A.M./P.M. Upon my arrival at the station, I proceeded to inspect and then clean the entire station including *Stairway S-6* and left it *in good condition*. I swept and cleaned that part of the station at about *11:00* A.M./P.M., the same as I do on every tour of duty and cleaned and inspected it again at about *2:00* A.M./P.M. before I went off duty. Did you inspect scene after accident? *Yes* If you did so, give time and condition.
    Date: *Feb. 27* Time: *11:45* A.M./P.M. Condition: *Clean and in good condition*
Weather Conditions *Clear*
Was there any snow or ice on the street surface? *No*
Was there any snow or ice on the part of the station involved in accident? *No*
Were there any defects or obstructions at place of accident? *No*
REMARKS: (Here give details as to conditions existing and all you know about this accident. *I saw a passenger lose his balance while descending Stairway S-6 and fall down the steps. He bruised his face. I inspected the stairway at 11:45 A.M. and found it clean and in good condition.*
Did you see the accident? *Yes*
Date report was signed by you: *Feb. 27*
FULL NAME: *John Brown* ADDRESS: *154 E. 18th St., N.Y., N.Y., Apt. 3C*

1. The accident occurred on
   A. Stairway N-6
   B. Northbound platform
   C. Southbound platform
   D. Stairway S-6

2. The stairway where the accident occurred was cleaned at
   A. 8:00 A.M.   B. 11:00 A.M.   C. 11:45 A.M.   D. 4:00 P.M.

3. Part I of the Cleaning Report may be filled out by any of the following employees EXCEPT the
   A. Station Supervisor
   B. Cleaner
   C. Railroad Clerk
   D. Claim Investigator

4. The accident to the passenger took place at
   A. 11:00 A.M.   B. 11:30 A.M.   C. 11:45 P.M.   D. 2:00 P.M.

5. Part II of the Cleaning Report was made out by the
   A. Assistant Station Supervisor
   B. Station Supervisor
   C. Cleaner
   D. Railroad Clerk

6. What was the pass number of the Cleaner?
   A. 323751   B. 372351   C. 327351   D. 327531

Question 7.

DIRECTIONS: Question 7 is to be answered SOLELY on the basis of the following information and the chart which appears on the following page.

As a supervisor, you have assigned Police Communications Technician Newhardt to work ERS for the day. During the tour, he received the calls listed below:

1. Spanish assist
2. Report of a fire at 366 East 66th Street, Apt. 9
3. Request for the 14th Precinct's address and telephone number
4. Request for an ambulance for an E.D.P. in front of 1717 Broadway
5. Fire Department test call
6. Series of tapping (2-3) from ERS box 2514

Near the end of the tour (1520 hours), you inspect his ERS log, and you notice that he has failed to complete certain information.

3 (#2)

EMERGENCY REPORTING SYSTEM LOG

DATE: _March 21_ BOROUGH: _Manhattan_
TOUR: _0800 x 1600_ POSITION: _POS 10_

	A	B	C	D	E	F	G	H	I	J	K	L	M	N
				\multicolumn{6}{c}{TYPE OF CALL}						
	TIME	BOX #	CPR#	PRAU	INFO	TEST	NA	MISC	INPUT	JOB #	CODE SIGNALS	INCIDENT LOCATION	EMP ASS.	FINAL DISP
1	1430	3691	001					✓				Referred to Spanish		
2	1436	4266	001							52611		366 E. 66 St.	23A	91
3	1439		001											
4	1445		001									1717 Broadway	34B	90Z
5		4444	001											
6	1449	2514	001						✓				26A	93C
7														
8														
9														
10														
11														
12														
13														
14	.													
15														
16			TOTALS								VERIFIED BY_____ SUPERVISOR'S SIGNATURE			

7. Which of the following series of letters and numbers represents information omitted in the log?
   A. A5, B4, J5, M1, G16, D16, I4, F16, E3, J6, K2, G7, M4, N6, B2, L1, M2, I1, I16
   B. A5, B4, E4, K9, J6, M6, L1, M2, B5, L3, I5, C6, B3, L6, M6, L5, G6, I16
   C. A5, B4, J5, K4, E3, G5, K6, I4, I2, K2, K6, D16, B2, L1, M2, I1, G6, I16
   D. A5, B3, B4, E3, F5, J4, K2, K4, J6, K6, L6, E16, F16, H16, I16, I4, I2, D16, G16

7.____

8. Assume that the Spring system fails and all Bronx operators are told by Supervising Dispatcher Shelton that a Backup Slip Operation will be in effect. Police Communications Technician Jordan then receives a call over the Emergency Reporting System indicating a call from fire box 7215. A Mrs. Smith is on the line reporting a heavy smoke condition in her third floor hallway at 6773 Dayton Drive. Operator Jordan disengages the call with Mrs. Smith and proceeds to connect to the Bronx fire operator. Fire Operator 737 accepts the information and advises Operator Jordan that a unit will be sent, although there have been numerous unfounded alarms at this location in the past. Operator Jordan then gives the slip to Supervising Dispatcher Shelton, who is passing by her position. The slip is shown on the following page.

8.____

4 (#2)

[Communications Division Incident Report form showing:
- INCIDENT ADDRESS: SPRING AVE. – SUMMER PLC 6773 DAYTONA DRIVE
- I.Q. 7
- 59R HEAVY SMOKE CONDITION
- APT/FL: 3RD FLOOR HALL
- DATE: 0-4-2-4
- OPERATOR'S NO.: 005-25
- CALLER'S TELEPHONE NO.: NONE
- REMARKS: CHRONIC LOCATION
- PCT: 27]

After checking the slip, Supervising Dispatcher Shelton should return it to Operator Jordan and tell her that she omitted the
 A. caller's name, routing, fire box number, time, precinct
 B. fire box number, caller's name, fire operator's number, time
 C. fire operator's number, fire box number, sector, date
 D. fire box number, precinct, intersection, time

Questions 9-10.

DIRECTIONS: Questions 9 and 10 are to be answered SOLELY on the basis of the following information.

Police Communications Technicians must be able to identify and assign codes to the crimes described in the calls they receive. All crimes are coded by number and by priority. The priority code number indicates the seriousness of the crime. The lower the priority number, the more serious the crime.

Listed below is a chart of several crimes and their definitions. The corresponding crime code and priority code number are given.

CRIME	DEFINITION	CRIME CODE	PRIORITY CODE
Criminal Mischief	Occurs when a person intentionally damages another person's property	29	6
Harrassment	Occurs when a person intentionally annoys another person by striking, shoving, or kicking them without causing injury	27	8
Aggravated Harrassment	Occurs when a person intentionally annoys another person by using any form of communication	28	9
Theft of Service	Occurs when a person intentionally avoids payment for services given	25	7

9. Communications Technician Rogers received a call from Mrs. Freeman, who stated that her next door neighbor, whom she had an argument with, has thrown a rock through her apartment window. Which one of the following is the CORRECT crime code?   9.____
   A. 29 B. 28 C. 27 D. 25

10. Communications Technician Tucker received a call from a man who stated that he is a waiter at the Frontier Diner. He states that one of his customers was refusing to pay for his meal. Which one of the following is the CORRECT priority code number for this crime?   10.____
    A. 6 B. 7 C. 8 D. 9

Question 11.

DIRECTIONS: Question 11 is to be answered SOLELY on the basis of the information below and the form appearing on the following page

Election of Rate of Charge Against Annual and/or Sick Leave Balances
for Absence Due to Injury Sustained in the Performance of Official Duties

(Pursuant to Regulation 7.0 of the Leave Regulations for Employees Who are
Under the Career and Salary Plan)

> INSTRUCTIONS: The injured employee, or an authorized person acting in his behalf, should submit this election notice (in duplicate) to the head of his department or agency within the first seven calendar days of absence due to injury sustained in the performance of official duties.

I, _____, employed in _____
(Print name of injured employee)   (Print name of city department or agency)
in a position which is subject to the Leave Regulations for employees who are under the Career and Salary Plan, or any authorized agent, do hereby elect the option designated below, subject to the conditions attached thereto, as the one to be applied in determining the charge, if any, to be made against my annual and/or sick leave balances for absence due to injury sustained in the performance of my official duties.
(Check one option only)
   OPTION I: I elect to receive the difference between the amount of my weekly salary and the compensation rate, subject to the following conditions:
   (a) A pro-rated charge shall be made against my sick leave and/or annual leave balances equal to the number of working days of absence less the number of working days represented by the Worker's Compensation payments, and;
   (b) My accrued sick leave and/or annual leave balances, or such leave credits advanced to me in accordance with the Career and Salary Plan Leave Regulations, are adequate to meet the charges made against them for supplementary pay, and;
   (c) The injury sustained by me was not the result of my willful gross disobedience of safety rules or my willful failure to use a safety device, nor was I under the influence of alcohol or narcotics at the time of injury, nor did I willfully intend to bring about injury or death upon myself or another, and;

(d) Such medical examinations will be undergone by me as are requested by the Worker's Compensation Division of the Law Department and my agency, and when found fit for duty by said physicians, I shall return to my employment.

OPTION 2: I elect to receive Workmen's Compensation benefits in their entirety with no charge against sick leave and/or annual leave.

Injured Employee's Signature		Date
This shaded section should be completed only if the injured employee cannot sign and must designate an authorized person to sign in his behalf	Authorized designer's (print)	Relationship to injured employee
	Authorized designer's address	
	Authorized designer's signature	Date
	Witness' name (print)	
	Witness' address	
	Witness' signature	Date

Employing Department should forward duplicate copy to Worker's Compensation Division of Law Department

11. Lt. Perry is reviewing a DP2002 form (see the form on the previous page) that was prepared as a result of an agent's on-the-job injury. Which one of the following statements concerning this form is CORRECT?
    A. If all of the agent's sick leave and annual leave have been used up, only Option 1 may be selected.
    B. The person who signs as a witness must have seen the accident and must be willing to swear that the agent was not at fault.
    C. If the agent wishes to switch from Option 1 to Option 2 when sick leave and annual leave have been used up, both Option 1 and Option 2 should be checked.
    D. An agent with sufficient sick leave and annual leave who wishes to continue receiving a regular paycheck should choose Option 1.

11.____

7 (#2)

Question 12.

DIRECTIONS: Question 12 is to be answered SOLELY on the basis of the following form.

EMPLOYEE'S NOTICE OF INJURY

ANSWER ALL QUESTIONS FULLY. THIS IS YOUR NOTICE TO YOUR EMPLOYER OF INJURY ON THE JOB. PRINT OR WRITE LEGIBLY.

Full name of injured person _Mary_   _M_   _Doe_
(First)   (Middle)   (Last)
Address _110 Finkel Road_
Employee's S.S. No. _172-00-1001_   Date of Birth _10/20/65_
Name of employer   CITY OF NEW YORK – DEPARTMENT OF _Transportation_
Date of accident _5/6/15_   Hour _10:15_ A.M. _____ P.M.
Exact location where accident happened _1st Ave and E. 57th St. Northwest Corner_

How did accident happen? (Describe fully) _While walking on 1st Ave. and E. 57th St., I stepped into a pothole, fell, and sprained my right ankle and my left wrist_

Nature and extent of injury _Sprained left ankle and left wrist_

Did you inform your superior of this accident? _Yes_   Date _5/6/20_
Name such person _Lt. Fudd_
Names and addresses of witnesses _Lt. Fudd   182 Mulholland Dr., N.Y. 11726_

Date _5/6/15_   (Sign here) _Mary Doe_
THIS IS NOT A CLAIM FORM. A CLAIM FORM MAY BE SECURED AT ANY OFFICE OF THE STATE WORKER'S COMPENSATION BOARD

12. On May 6, Traffic Enforcement Agent Mary M. Doe, SS# 172-00-1001, had an accident at 10:15 A.M. while patrolling her sector. She was walking south on the east side of 1st Avenue and was about to cross East 57th Street when she tripped on a pothole and fell, spraining her right ankle and left wrist. Lt. Fudd was on the scene at the time and witnessed the accident. After the agent received medical attention, Lt. Fudd reviews the Employee's Notice of Injury form shown on the previous page, including the reports of the

    I. Description of the injury
    II. Date and time of the accident
    III. Location where the accident occurred
    IV. Employee's Social Security number

Which of the above entries are correct and which are incorrect?
_____ are correct, but _____ are incorrect.

  A. I and II; III and IV
  B. I and III; II and IV
  C. II and IV; I and III
  D. III and IV; I and II

12.____

Question 13.

DIRECTIONS: Question 13 is to be answered SOLELY on the basis of the form which is shown below.

DEPT. OF TRANSPORTATION
TRAFFIC CONTROL DIVISION-ENFORCEMENT
DAILY FIELD PATROL SHEET

I - AGENT IDENTIFICATION INFORMATION

NAME				RANK	BADGE NO.
Jones, Alice				TEA 1	007

TAX REG NO	CMD	ENF GRP	SQD	MO.	DAY	YR
235719	6Q3	F7P	G	05	30	15

MULTIPLE PAGE CHECK

PAGE	OF

PRE=PRINTED ADHESIVE LABEL TO BE ATTACHED HERE BY LT. OR INDIVIDUAL AGENT

II - MISCELLANEOUS INFORMATION

POST or SECTOR	POST CHANGE
6301	

MEAL	VEHICLE NO.	PORTABLE NO.
1100	-	666

III - TIME & ATTENDANCE

REGULAR TOUR		OVERTIME TOUR		TOTAL HOURS	ROO
FROM	TO	FROM	TO		
07:00	03:00			08:00	X

IV - DETAILED ACTIVITIES

ACTIVITY DESCRIPTION	TOW VOUCHER NO.	ACTIVITY CODE	TIME ARRIVED	TIME DEPARTED	POST CODE	SUMS ISSD	TOWS
DO		DOAD	7:00	07:15			
TRAVEL		TRVL	07:15	08:00			
On 7 Av from 3 St TO 8 St		ISSP	08:00	09:00	6301	8	
PERSONAL		PR5N	09:00	09:15			
On 7 Av from 3 St TO 8 St		ISSP	09:15	11:00	6301	12	
MEAL		MEAL	11:00	12:45			
On 7 Av from 3 St TO 8 St		ISSP	12:45	01:30	6301	8	
TRAVEL		TRVL	01:30	02:15			
DO		DOAD	02:15	03:00			

TOTAL SUMMONSES ISSUED/VEHICLES TOWED	28

VII - SPECIAL SUMMONS ACTIVITIES

POST CODE	COMLO	MISC 1	MISC 2	MISC 3	MISC 4
TOTAL					

V - SUMMONSES USED

STARTING SUMMONS NO.	ENDING SUMMONS NO.	TOTAL
978676763	97867706	25
978677015	978677033	3
		28

VIII - SIGNATURES

AGENT	Alice Jones
LL	Thomas Smart
LL	

VI – ERROR SUMMONSES & MOVING VIOLATIONS

TYPE	CODE	SUMMONS NO.
E	E	97867742

TIME/DATE STAMP TO FIELD	TIME/DATE STAMP FROM FIELD

13. Lt. Howard is reviewing Traffic Enforcement Agent Jones' Daily Field Patrol Sheet (TCD-210), the front side of which is shown on the preceding page. The Lieutenant checks the following entries:
    I. Activity Codes
    II. Summonses Used
    III. Signatures
    IV. Post Codes
    V. Time and Attendance

    The Lieutenant should notice that there are errors in _____, but not in _____.
    A. I and IV; II, III, and V
    B. II and III; I, IV, and V
    C. II and V; I, III, and IV
    D. I, III, and V; II and IV

13.____

Questions 14-20.

DIRECTIONS: Questions 14 through 20 are to be answered SOLELY on the basis of the numbered boxes on the Arrest Report and paragraph below.

ARREST REPORT

1. Arrest Number	2. Precinct of Arrest		3. Date/Time of Arrest		4. Defendant's Name	5. Defendant's Address
6. Defendant's Date of Birth	7. Sex	8. Race	9. Height	10. Weight	11. Location of Arrest	12. Date & Time of Occurrence
13. Location of Occurrence	14. Complaint Number		15. Victim's Name		16. Victim's Address	17. Victim's Date of Birth
18. Precinct of Complaint	19. Arresting Officer's Name		20. Shield Number		21. Assigned Unit Precinct	22. Date of Complaint

On Friday, December 13, at 11:45 P.M., while leaving a store at 235 Spring Street, Grace O'Connell, a white female, 5'2", 130 lbs., was approached by a white male, 5'11", 200 lbs., who demanded her money and jewelry. As the man ran and turned down River Street, Police Officer William James, Shield Number 31724, assigned to the 14th Precinct, gave chase and apprehended him in front of 523 River Street. The prisoner, Gerald Grande, who resides at 17 Water Street, was arrested at 12:05 A.M., was charged with robbery, and taken to the 13th Precinct, where he was assigned Arrest Number 53048. Miss O'Connell, who resides at 275 Spring St., was given Complaint Number 82460.

14. On the basis of the Arrest Report and paragraph above, the CORRECT entry for Box Number 3 should be
    A. 11:45 P.M., 12/13
    B. 11:45 P.M., 12/14
    C. 12:05 A.M., 12/13
    D. 12:05 A.M., 12/14

14.____

15. On the basis of the Arrest Report and paragraph above, the CORRECT entry for Box Number 21 should be
    A. 13th Precinct
    B. 14th Precinct
    C. Mounted Unit
    D. 32nd Precinct

15.____

10 (#2)

16. On the basis of the Arrest Report and paragraph above, the CORRECT entry for Box Number 11 should be
    A. 235 Spring St.
    B. 523 River St.
    C. 275 Spring St.
    D. 17 Water St.

16.____

17. On the basis of the Arrest Report and paragraph above, the CORRECT entry for Box Number 2 should be
    A. 13th Precinct
    B. 14th Precinct
    C. Mounted Unit
    D. 32nd Precinct

17.____

18. On the basis of the Arrest Report and paragraph above, the CORRECT entry for Box Number 13 should be
    A. 523 River St.
    B. 17 Water St.
    C. 275 Spring St.
    D. 235 Spring St.

18.____

19. On the basis of the Arrest Report and paragraph above, the CORRECT entry for Box Number 14 should be
    A. 53048
    B. 31724
    C. 12/13
    D. 82460

19.____

20. On the basis of the Arrest Report and paragraph above, the CORRECT entry for Box Number 13 should be
    A. 275 Spring St.
    B. 523 River St.
    C. 235 Spring St.
    D. 17 Water St.

20.____

KEY (CORRECT ANSWERS)

1.	D	11.	D
2.	B	12.	C
3.	B	13.	C
4.	B	14.	D
5.	C	15.	B
6.	C	16.	B
7.	D	17.	A
8.	B	18.	D
9.	A	19.	D
10.	B	20.	C

READING COMPREHENSION
UNDERSTANDING AND INTERPRETING WRITTEN MATERIAL

EXAMINATION SECTION
TEST 1

DIRECTIONS: Each question or incomplete statement is followed by several suggested answers or completions. Select the one that BEST answers the question or completes the statement. *PRINT THE LETTER OF THE CORRECT ANSWER IN THE SPACE AT THE RIGHT.*

Questions 1-3.

DIRECTIONS: Questions 1 through 3 are to be answered in accordance with the following passage.

Terrazzo flooring will last a very long time if it is cared for properly. Lacquers, shellac, or varnish preparations should never be used on terrazzo. Soap cleaners are not recommended since they dull the appearance of the floor. Alkaline solutions are harmful, so a neutral cleaner or non-alkaline synthetic detergents will give best results. If the floor is very dirty, it may be necessary to scrub it. The same neutral cleaning solution should be used for scrubbing as for mopping. Scouring powder may be sprinkled at particularly dirty spots. Do not use steel wool for scrubbing. Small pieces of steel filings left on the floor will rust and dis-color the terrazzo. Non-woven nylon or open-mesh fabric abrasive pads are suitable for scrubbing terrazzo floors.

1. According to the passage above, the BEST cleaning agent for terrazzo flooring is a(n)   1.____

    A. soap cleaner
    B. varnish preparation
    C. neutral cleaner
    D. alkaline solution

2. According to the passage above, terrazzo floors should NOT be scrubbed with   2.____

    A. non-woven nylon abrasive pads
    B. steel wool
    C. open-mesh fabric abrasive pads
    D. scouring powder

3. As used in the passage above, the word *discolor* means MOST NEARLY   3.____

    A. crack   B. scratch   C. dissolve   D. stain

Questions 4-7.

DIRECTIONS: Questions 4 through 7 are to be answered in accordance with the information given in the following passage.

MOPPING FLOORS

When mopping hardened cement floors, either painted or unpainted, a soap and water mixture should be used. This should be made by dissolving half a cup of soft soap in a pail of hot water. It is not desirable, however, under any circumstances, to use a soap and water mixture on cement floors that are not hardened. For mopping this type of floor, it is recommended that the cleaning agent be made up of 2 ounces of laundry soda mixed in a pail of water.

Soaps are not generally used on hard tile floors because slippery films may build up on the floor. It is generally recommended that these floors be mopped using a pail of hot water in which has been mixed 2 ounces of washing powder for each gallon of water. The floors should then be rinsed thoroughly.

After the mopping is finished, proper care should be taken of the mop. This is done by first cleaning the mop in clear warm water. Then, it should be wrung out, after which the strands of the mop should be untangled. Finally, the mop should be hung by its handle to dry.

4. According to the above passage, you should NEVER use a soap and water mixture when mopping _____ floors.

    A. hardened cement
    B. painted
    C. unhardened cement
    D. unpainted

5. According to the above passage, using laundry soda mixed in a pail of water as a cleaning agent is recommended for

    A. all floors
    B. all floors except hard tile floors
    C. some cement floors
    D. linoleum floor coverings *only*

6. According to the above passage, the GENERALLY recommended mixture for mopping hard tile floors is _____ of hot water.

    A. 1/2 cup of soft soap for each gallon
    B. 1/2 cup of soft soap in a pail
    C. 2 ounces of washing powder in a pail
    D. 2 ounces of washing powder for each gallon

7. According to the above passage, the PROPER care of a mop after it is used includes

    A. cleaning it in clear cold water and hanging it by its handle to dry
    B. wringing it out, untangling and drying it
    C. untangling its strands before wringing it out
    D. untangling its strands while cleaning it in clear water

Questions 8-15.

DIRECTIONS: Questions 8 through 15 are to be answered ONLY in accordance with the following paragraph.

Many custodial foremen have discovered through experience that there are economies to be *realized* by using discretion when ordering items which are similar to each other. For example, it may be cheaper to order a *Sponge block, cellulose, WET SIZE: 6 in. x 4 3/4 in. x APPROXIMATELY 34 inches long* at $7.00 than it is to order separate *Sponges, cellulose, wet size: 2 in. x 4 in. x 6 in.* at 60¢. It does not pay to *over-order* on floor wax which may turn sour if not used soon enough. An average size college building cannot afford to have extra 30-inch floor brooms costing $19.75 each stored *on the shelf* for a couple of years or to let moths destroy the hair in such brooms if proper safeguards are not used.

8. According to the above passage, the items mentioned which are *similar* are   8._____

    A. floor brooms B. sponges
    C. floor waxes   D. moths

9. As used in the above paragraph, the term *over-order* means to   9._____

    A. order again   B. back order
    C. order too little D. order too much

10. Of the items for which prices are given in the above paragraph, the MOST expensive one is the   10._____

    A. 30-inch floor broom
    B. 6 in. x 4 3/4 in. x 34 in. sponge block
    C. 2 in. x 4 in. x 6 in. sponge
    D. floor wax

11. As used in the above paragraph, the word *realized* means MOST NEARLY   11._____

    A. obtained   B. lost   C. equalized   D. cheapened

12. According to the above paragraph, the one of the following which may be damaged by moths is the   12._____

    A. floor broom   B. sponge
    C. cellulose   D. wool cloth

13. As used in the above paragraph, the term *wet size* means   13._____

    A. the chemical treatment given to sponges
    B. the amount of water the sponge can hold
    C. that the sponges must be kept moist at all times
    D. that the measurements given were taken when the sponges were wet

14. As used in the above paragraph, the word *at* means   14._____

    A. near   B. arrived   C. each   D. new

15. As used in the above paragraph, the word *approximately* means   15._____

    A. exactly   B. about   C. economical   D. tan

Questions 16-17.

DIRECTIONS: Questions 16 and 17 are to be answered in accordance with the following paragraph.

Painting is done to preserve surfaces; and unless the surface is properly prepared, good preservation will not be possible. Apply paint only to clean dry surfaces. After a surface has been scaled, which means that all loose paint and rust are removed by chipping, scraping, and wire brushing, be sure all dust and dirt are completely removed.

16. According to the above paragraph, the MAIN purpose of painting a wall is to _____ the wall.   16.____

    A. clean
    B. waterproof
    C. protect
    D. remove dust from

17. According to the above paragraph,   17.____

    A. chipping, scraping, and wire brushing are the only methods permitted for cleaning surfaces
    B. painting is effective only when the surface is clean
    C. scaling refers only to the removal of rust
    D. paint may be applied on wet surfaces

Questions 18-21.

DIRECTIONS: Questions 18 through 21 are to be answered SOLELY on the basis of the following paragraph.

All cleaning agents and supplies should be kept in a central storeroom which should be kept locked and only the custodian, store-keeper, and foreman should have keys. Shelving should be provided for the smaller items while barrels containing scouring powder or other bulk material should be set on the floor or on special cradles. Each compartment in the shelves should be marked plainly and only the item indicated stored therein. Each barrel should also be marked plainly. It may also be desirable to keep special items such as electric lamps, flashlight batteries, etc. in a locked cabinet or separate room to which only the custodian and the night building foreman have keys.

18. According to the above paragraph, scouring powder   18.____

    A. should be kept on shelves
    B. comes in one-pound cans
    C. should be kept in a locked cabinet
    D. is a bulk material

19. According to the above paragraph,   19.____

    A. the storekeeper should not be entrusted with the safekeeping of light bulbs
    B. flashlight batteries should be stored in barrels
    C. the central storeroom should be kept locked
    D. only special items should be stored under lock and key

20. According to the above paragraph,   20.____

    A. each shelf compartment should contain at least four different items
    B. barrels must be stored in cradles
    C. all items stored should be in marked compartments
    D. crates of light bulbs should be stored in cradles

21. As used in the above paragraph, the word *cradle* means a   21.____

    A. dolly   B. support
    C. doll's bed   D. hand truck

Questions 22-25.

DIRECTIONS: Questions 22 through 25 are to be answered SOLELY on the basis of the following paragraph.

There are on the market many cleaning agents for which amazing claims are made. Chemical analysis shows that the majority of them are well-known chemicals slightly modified and packaged and sold under various trade names. For that reason, the agents which have been selected for your use are those whose cleaning properties are well-known and whose use can be standardized. It is obviously undesirable to offer too wide a selection as that would be confusing to the cleaner, but a sufficient number must be provided so that a satisfactory agent is available for each task.

22. According to the above paragraph,   22.____

    A. there are few cleaning agents on the market
    B. there are no really good cleaning agents on the market
    C. cleaning agents are sold under several different brand names
    D. all cleaning agents are the same

23. According to the above paragraph,   23.____

    A. all cleaning agents should be chemically analyzed before use
    B. the best cleaning agents are those for which no claims are made by the manufacturer
    C. different cleaning agents may be needed for different tasks
    D. all cleaning agents have been standardized by the federal government

24. As used in the above paragraph, the word *amazing* means   24.____

    A. illegal   B. untrue
    C. astonishing   D. specific

25. As used in the above paragraph, the word *modified* means   25.____

    A. changed   B. refined   C. labelled   D. diluted

KEY (CORRECT ANSWERS)

1. C
2. B
3. D
4. C
5. C

6. D
7. B
8. B
9. D
10. A

11. A
12. A
13. D
14. C
15. B

16. C
17. B
18. D
19. C
20. C

21. B
22. C
23. C
24. C
25. A

TEST 2

Questions 1-3.

DIRECTIONS: Questions 1 through 3 are to be answered in accordance with the following passage. Each question or incomplete statement is followed by several suggested answers or completions. Select the one that BEST answers the question or completes the statement. *PRINT THE LETTER OF THE CORRECT ANSWER IN THE SPACE AT THE RIGHT.*

The method of cleaning which should generally be used is the space assignment method. Under this method, the buildings to be cleaned are divided into different sections. Within each section, each crew of Custodial Assistants is assigned to do one particular cleaning job. For example, within a section, one crew may be assigned to cleaning offices, another to scrubbing floors, a third to collecting trash, and so on. Other methods which may be used are the post assignment method and the gang cleaning method. Under the post assignment method, a Custodial Assistant is assigned to one area of a building and performs all cleaning jobs in that area. This method is seldom used except where buildings are so small and distant from each other that it is not economical to use the space assignment method. Under the gang cleaning method, a Custodial Foreman takes a number of Custodial Assistants through a section of the building. These Custodial Assistants work as a group and complete the various cleaning jobs as they go. This method is generally used only where the building contains very large open areas.

1. According to the passage above, under the space assignment method, each crew GENERALLY

    A. works as a group and does a variety of different cleaning jobs
    B. is assigned to one area and performs all cleaning jobs in that area
    C. does one particular cleaning job within a section of a building
    D. follows the Custodial Foreman through a building containing large, open areas

1.____

2. According to the passage above, the post assignment method is used MOSTLY where the buildings to be cleaned are _____ in size and situated _____.

    A. large; close together   B. small; close together
    C. large; far apart   D. small; far apart

2.____

3. As used in the passage above, the word *economical* means MOST NEARLY

    A. thrifty   B. agreed   C. unusual   D. wasteful

3.____

Questions 4-25.

DIRECTIONS: Each question consists of a statement. You are to indicate whether the statement is TRUE (T) or FALSE (F). *PRINT THE LETTER OF THE CORRECT ANSWER IN THE SPACE AT THE RIGHT.*

Questions 4-8.

DIRECTIONS: Questions 4 through 8 are to be answered in accordance with the information given in the following paragraph.

The removal of fine, loose dirt or dust from desks, chairs, filing cabinets, tables, and other furniture or office machines is called dusting. A yard of clean soft cloth, folded into a pad about nine inches square, is best for dusting. The cloth should be dry since oil or water on the cloth may streak the surface that is being dusted. When dusting a desk, care must be taken to put back in the same place any papers that were lifted or moved to one side. Thorough dusting of an office is important in order for the office to look neat and for the health of the people who work in that office.

4. The removal of fine, loose dirt or dust from furniture or office machines is called dusting.   4.____

5. A pad of cloth twelve inches square is best for dusting.   5.____

6. A dry cloth will streak the surface that is being dusted.   6.____

7. Papers that have been lifted or moved to one side when dusting a desk should be put back in the same place.   7.____

8. It is not important to dust an office thoroughly.   8.____

Questions 9-18.

DIRECTIONS: Questions 9 through 18 are to be answered in accordance with the information given in the following paragraphs.

WASHING OF WALLS

The washing of walls is important since wall-cleaning costs are an expensive item in the operating cost of building maintenance.

There is a right and a wrong way to wash walls. Streaks may be caused by water running down the dry wall below the place where one is working. This can be prevented by first wetting a section of the wall with water, starting at the bottom and working up before starting the actual washing operation with cleaning solution. Then, if the water runs down the wet wall, there will be almost no streaking. While washing a wall, the temperature should be reasonably low so that the water will not dry on the wall and cause streaks. Once the dirt on the wall is moistened, the wall must be kept wet until the dirt is removed. The washing of walls should be done with good sponges. One sponge should be for cleaning on the dirty wall and one for rinsing.

When working with the cleaning solution, start at the top of the wall and use a circular motion of the sponge and hand. Work across a given section first to the right and then to the left, and so on down to the base.

After the dirt has been removed, take clean, cool water and a clean sponge and go over the wall to be sure that it is perfectly clean and that no traces of the cleaning solution remain on the wall. Even clean water drying unevenly on a wall will cause slight streaks which become noticeable on the walls.

9. The amount of money spent to wash walls is a very small part in the expenses of running a building.   9.____

10. To prevent streaks when washing a wall, an employee should FIRST wet the wall, starting at the top and working down to the base of a wall. 10.____

11. If a wall is wet in the right way, there will be practically no streaks caused by water running down the wet wall. 11.____

12. If the walls are washed when the room is hot, streaks can be caused by water drying too quickly. 12.____

13. Once a dirty wall is made wet with water, it should be dried completely before the dirt is removed. 13.____

14. To wash walls properly, an employee should use at least two good sponges. 14.____

15. When washing with the cleaning solution, start at the bottom of the wall and work to the top, using a circular motion of the hand and sponge. 15.____

16. When washing with the cleaning solution, the CORRECT method is to work across each part of the wall going first to the left and ending on the right. 16.____

17. After the wall has been washed with the cleaning solution, it must be gone over again with clean water to remove any solution which is left on the wall. 17.____

18. When clean water is used to wash a wall, streaks will never appear, even if the wall dries unevenly. 18.____

Questions 19-25.

DIRECTIONS: Questions 19 through 25 are to be answered in accordance with the information given in the following passage.

CLEANING ELECTRIC LIGHT FIXTURES

A room may be dark not because there are not enough light fixtures but because the globes are dirty. As frequently as found necessary, and at least once a year, each globe on a light fixture should be taken down and carefully washed. It should be cleaned by using a solution of warm water to which has been added about two tablespoons full of washing soda for each 10 quarts of water. The globe must be thoroughly dried before it is put back or it is liable to crack from the heat of the lamp. At the time the globe is washed, the metal parts of the fixture should be wiped with a rag dampened in plain warm water. Most metal fixtures have been lacquered, and any cleaning solution would tend to destroy the lacquer. The electric light bulb should be unscrewed from the fixture and wiped with a slightly damp cloth. If it is burned out, it should be replaced at this time.

19. Dirty light globes will reduce the amount of light in a room. 19.____

20. Light globes should be cleaned only when the attendant replaces a burned out light bulb in a fixture. 20.____

21. To clean light globes, a solution of cold water and ordinary household ammonia should be used. 21.____

22. If a light globe is not completely dry when it is put back on a fixture after washing, the heat from the light bulb can break the globe. 22.____

23. The metal parts of a light fixture should be cleaned by using a dry rag to which has been added a few drops of a cleaning solution. 23.____

24. Most metal light fixtures have a coating of lacquer on them. 24.____

25. To clean a light bulb in a fixture, it should be unscrewed and wiped with a damp cloth. 25.____

KEY (CORRECT ANSWERS)

1. C
2. D
3. A
4. T
5. F

6. F
7. T
8. F
9. F
10. F

11. T
12. T
13. F
14. T
15. F

16. F
17. T
18. F
19. T
20. F

21. F
22. T
23. F
24. T
25. T

ARITHMETICAL REASONING
EXAMINATION SECTION
TEST 1

DIRECTIONS: Each question or incomplete statement is followed by several suggested answers or completions. Select the one that BEST answers the question or completes the statement. *PRINT THE LETTER OF THE CORRECT ANSWER IN THE SPACE AT THE RIGHT.*

1. Assume that a room measures 12'6" x 11'4". Its area is MOST NEARLY _____ sq. ft.   1._____
   A. 138 B. 139
   C. 140 D. 142

2. The SMALLEST subdivision found on the ordinary six-foot wooden rule is   2._____
   A. 1/32"   B. 1/16"   C. 1/8"   D. 1/4"

3. The sum of the following numbers, 6 1/4, 5 3/16, 7 1/2, 8 1/8, and 7 5/16, is   3._____
   A. 34 1/4   B. 34 5/16   C. 34 3/8   D. 34 7/16

4. 92796 divided by 376 is MOST NEARLY   4._____
   A. 245   B. 247   C. 249   D. 251

5. Assume that an inspector will average 8 inspections per day. The number of days it will take seven inspectors to complete a total of 1,344 inspections at the same average rate is   5._____
   A. 24   B. 26   C. 28   D. 30

6. The MAXIMUM number of 3" x 5" pieces that can be cut from one sheet of 17" x 22" paper is   6._____
   A. 20   B. 21   C. 22   D. 23

7. Suppose you are told to print a year's supply of a form. If 1,500 copies are used each month and the form is printed three up on an 8 1/2" x 14" sheet and cut to 4 1/2" x 8 1/2", how many 8 1/2" x 14" sheets are needed (disregarding waste)?   7._____
   A. 3,000   B. 4,500   C. 5,400   D. 6,000

8. The MAXIMUM number of 4" x 5" pieces that can be cut from five 500-sheet packages of 16" x 21" paper is   8._____
   A. 30,000   B. 40,000   C. 50,000   D. 60,000

9. The manager of the project has asked you to compute the cost of 175 feet of electric wire needed for an installation in the project community room. This wire is listed in the catalog in 1,000-foot coils, each coil weighing 32 pounds and costing $1.14 a pound. The cost of the wire to be used is MOST NEARLY   9._____
   A. $4.35   B. $5.94   C. $6.24   D. $6.39

10. One section of a project containing 800 apartments was constructed at a cost of $116,000 per apartment. The two remaining sections of the project, containing 625 apartments each, are still to be built.
In order that the average construction cost per apartment for the entire project will not exceed $130,000, the cost per apartment in the two sections still to be built should be APPROXIMATELY

   A. $131,000   B. $135,000   C. $139,000   D. $140,000

11. A certain project contains 57 two-room apartments (for 2 persons), 305 three-room apartments (for 3 persons), 309 four-room apartments (for 4 persons), 104 five-room apartments (for 4 persons), 197 five-room apartments (for 5 persons), and 52 five-room apartments (for 6 persons).
The percentage of 4-person apartments in this project is between

   A. 10 and 19.9   B. 20 and 29.9
   C. 30 and 39.9   D. 40 and 49.9

12. Assume that each year the value of a certain project depreciates 2 1/2% of its original value.
At the end of the third year, its value, after depreciation, is $6,734,900. The original value was MOST NEARLY

   A. $7,252,000   B. $7,253,000
   C. $7,280,000   D. $7,290,000

13. A housing project with A apartments contains a total of R rooms. The total number of residents is N.
The number of residents per apartment is expressed by

   A. N/A   B. R/A   C. A/N   D. N/R

14. A unit of ten housing assistants has been assigned the job of interviewing 1,800 applicants. They are each able to do two interviews an hour. After the job is one-third done, an improvement in the procedure is put into effect which makes it possible to save 25% of the time.
The number of 7-hour days required for the entire job is MOST NEARLY

   A. 10   B. 11   C. 12   D. 13

15. Assume that 135,200 new applications were received in a certain year for the 9,500 apartments made available in new projects. In addition, 32,900 old applications were reviewed for eligibility for the new apartments. Of these, 49,300 new and 9,400 old applicants were found eligible.
The percentage of eligible applicants who will NOT receive an apartment is

   A. under 75%   B. between 75% and 80%
   C. between 80% and 85%   D. over 85%

16. A project tenant who is a cabdriver works on a commission basis, receiving 42 1/2% of the fares. In addition, his earnings from tips are valued at 29% of the commissions. If his average monthly fares equal $520, then his annual earnings are

   A. between $3,000 and $3,400   B. between $3,400 and $3,800
   C. between $3,800 and $4,200   D. over $4,200

17. A project tenant's earning record for the year is as follows: up to January 15, unemployed; continuously employed for the rest of the year; from Monday, January 16, $430 a week; from Monday, April 3, $390 a week; from Monday, October 2, $450 a week.
This tenant's yearly income is MOST NEARLY

    A. $15,000   B. $17,500   C. $21,000   D. $22,500

18. In a certain city in 2000, the average cost for constructing one apartment of a public housing project was $127,500, an increase of 4% over 1999.
The cost of constructing a project of 1,500 apartments in 2000 was more than in 1999 by an amount which is MOST NEARLY

    A. $6,000,000   B. $6,150,000
    C. $7,400,000   D. $7,650,000

Questions 19-20.

DIRECTIONS: Questions 19 and 20 are to be answered SOLELY on the basis of the following paragraph.

A housing development has 450 apartments. The average weekly rent is $134.50 per apartment. The average amount of subsidy money added to the average weekly rent (to meet the total operating costs) is $68.00. Since the time when the amount of the subsidy was determined, operating costs for the development have increased by $3,960.00 per week.

19. If the subsidy is increased by 6%, what INCREASE in the average weekly rental will be necessary to meet monthly operating costs?

    A. $3.40   B. $4.72
    C. $8.80   D. No increase

20. What is the NEW total weekly operating cost per apartment?

    A. $76.80   B. $143.30   C. $211.30   D. $242.10

21. In a certain housing project, the average income of tenant families is $19,400 per annum and the average rent per apartment is $360 per month.
If the average income increases 12% in a year while the average rent of an apartment increases 15%, how much MORE money will the average family have in a year after paying rent?

    A. $677.60   B. $1,680.00   C. $2,241.60   D. $4,968.00

22. A certain housing project has 1,860 tenant families. It has two playgrounds, both rectangular in shape. One measures 104 feet by 45 feet; the other is 74 feet by 53 feet.
The number of square feet of playground space per family in this project is MOST NEARLY

    A. 3   B. 5   C. 7   D. 9

23. A particular housing project has 1,460 occupied apartments. If there are 12 new tenants in January, 14 in February, and 16 in March, the turnover rate for the first quarter of the year is MOST NEARLY

   A. 2.9%   B. 3.2%   C. 3.5%   D. 3.8%

24. In 2009, the cost of refrigerator repairs and maintenance at a certain housing project was $2,700 more than in 2008, representing an increase of 18%. A further increase at the same rate is expected in 2010.
   The cost of refrigerator repairs and maintenance in 2010 will be MOST NEARLY

   A. $6,000   B. $10,000   C. $18,000   D. $21,000

25. If a tenant earns $31,680 a year and his rent is 25% of his annual income, the amount of rent he pays each month is

   A. $660   B. $690   C. $720   D. $810

KEY (CORRECT ANSWERS)

1. D		11. D	
2. B		12. C	
3. C		13. A	
4. B		14. B	
5. A		15. C	
6. B		16. B	
7. D		17. C	
8. B		18. C	
9. D		19. B	
10. C		20. C	

21. B
22. B
23. A
24. D
25. A

SOLUTIONS TO PROBLEMS

1. Area = (12.5')(11 1/3') = 141 2/3 sq.ft. ≈ 142 sq.ft.

2. 1/16" the smallest marking on a six-foot wooden ruler.

3. 6 1/4 + 5 3/16 + 7 1/2 + 8 1/8 + 7 5/16 = 33 22/16 = 34 3/8

4. 92,796 ÷ 376 ≈ 246.8 ≈ 247

5. 7 inspectors can do a total of 56 inspections per day. Then, 1344 ÷ 56 = 24 days

6.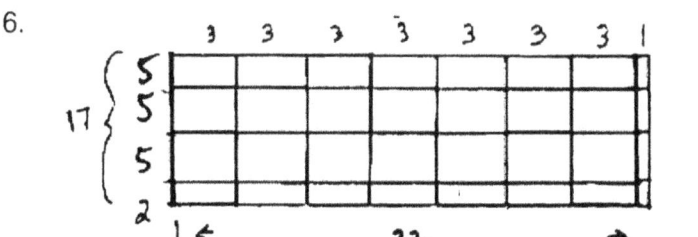

7. Each year, (1500)(12) = 18,000 forms are needed. Since 3 forms can fit on each sheet, 18,000 ÷ 3 = 6000 sheets are needed.

8. 16" ÷ 4" = 4 and 21" ÷ 5" rounds down to 4. Then, (4)(4) = 16 pieces of dimensions 4"x5" can be cut from each original 16"x21" piece of paper. For 2500 original sheets, we can cut (2500)(16) = 40,000 4"x5" pieces.

9. Let x = weight of the 175-ft. wire. x/175 = 32/1000. Solving, x = 5.6 lbs. The cost of this wire = (5.6)($1.14) = $6.38

10. Let x = cost per apartment for the remaining 1250 apartments. Then, [(800)($116,000)+1250x]/2050 < $130,000. Simplifying, $92,800,000 + 1250x < $266,500,000. Solving, x < $138,960 or approx. $139,000.

11. (309+104) ÷ (57+305+309+104+197+52) = 413/1024 = 40.33%

12. .925x = 6,734,900; x = 7,280,000

13. If A apartments contain N residents, the number of residents per apartment = N/A

14. (10)(2) = 20 applicants can be interviewed in 1 hour. Then, 600 ÷ 20 = 30 hours. The remaining 1200 applicants would normally require an additional 1200 ÷ 20 = 60 hours; however, the new procedure of interviewing these 1200 applicants will take (60)(.75) = 45 hours. Total time for all 1800 applicants = 30 + 45 = 75 hours. Finally, 75 ÷ 7 = 10.7 ≈ 11 days. (using 7 hours = 1 day)

15. 49,300 + 9,400 = 58,700 eligible applicants. Since only 9500 apartments are available, 49,200 eligible applicants will not receive an apartment. Finally, 49,200 ÷ 58,700 = 83.8%.

6 (#1)

16. If his monthly fare averages $520, he gets a commission of ($520)(.425) = $221 and tips of ($221)(.29) ~ $64. His annual earnings = (12)($221+$64) = $3420.

17. (11)($430) + (26)($390) + (13)($450) = $20,720 ≈ $21,000

18. The cost for one apartment in 1999 was $127,500 * 1.04 = $122,596. The cost difference per apartment from 1999 to 2000 was ~ $4904. For 1500 apartments, the additional cost was (1500)($4904) = $7,356,000 ~ $7,400,000.

19. $3960 ÷ 450 = $8.80 required increase per apartment to meet new operating costs. The increase in the subsidy = (.06)($68) = $4.08. The weekly rental increase necessary = $8.80 - $4.08 = $4.72

20. New operating cost per apartment (weekly) = $134.50 + $68 + $8.80 = $211.30

21. $19,400 - (12)($360) = $15,080. The new annual income = ($19,400)(1.12) = $21,728 and the new monthly rent = ($360X1.15) = $414. Then, $21,728 - (12)($414) = $16,760. Finally, $16,760 - $15,080 = $1680

22. (104)(45) + (74)(53) = 8602 sq.ft. Then, 8602 ÷ 1860 ≈ 5

23. (12+14+16) ÷ 1460 = 42/1460 ≈ 2.9%

24. The cost in 2008 was $2700 ÷ .18 = $15,000. Thus, the cost in 2009 was $15,000 + 2700 = $17,700. Finally, the cost in 2010 was ($17,700X1.18) = $20,886 ≈ $21,000

25. (.25)($31,680) = $7,920. Then, $7,920   12 = $660

TEST 2

DIRECTIONS: Each question or incomplete statement is followed by several suggested answers or completions. Select the one that BEST answers the question or completes the statement. *PRINT THE LETTER OF THE CORRECT ANSWER IN THE SPACE AT THE RIGHT.*

1. The area of the plot plan shown at the right is _____ square feet.
   A. 25,300
   B. 26,700
   C. 28,100
   D. 30,500

   (Plot plan dimensions: 270', 70', 155', 115', 150')

   1.____

2. A pump that removes 30 gallons of water per minute is pumping water from a cellar 30 feet x 50 feet covered with eight inches of water. One cubic foot of water equals 7.5 gallons of water.
   The number of minutes it will take to remove the eight inches of water from the cellar is

   A. 200   B. 225   C. 250   D. 275

   2.____

3. In order to clean an office with 20,000 sq.ft. of space in 4 hours using a standard of 900 sq.ft. per hour, the number of cleaners you should assign to do the job is MOST NEARLY

   A. 4   B. 6   C. 8   D. 10

   3.____

4. The area of a floor 35' wide and 45' long is, in square yards, MOST NEARLY

   A. 175   B. 262   C. 525   D. 1,575

   4.____

Questions 5-6.

DIRECTIONS: Questions 5 and 6 are to be answered on the basis of the following paragraph.

   A tenant in a housing development receives a semi-monthly public assistance check of $468 and pays a monthly rental of $284 from the proceeds. The tenant is about to begin paying $36 additional per month toward total rent arrears of $544. At the same time that the arrears payments begin, his semi-monthly check increases to $484.

5. What will be the TOTAL change in monthly net income after all rent payments?

   A. $12   B. $8   C. $4   D. No change

   5.____

6. If, instead of paying only $36 per month toward the arrears, the total increase in public assistance payments is used to increase arrears payments, how many months will it take the tenant to pay off the arrears? _____ months.

   A. 8   B. 10   C. 12   D. 14

   6.____

7. A tenant is offered two options in renewing a lease:
   (1) a one-year lease at a 10% increase in rent, or
   (2) a three-year lease at an 18% increase in rent.
   The tenant's current rent is $220 monthly.
   If the tenant takes the first option and continues to live in the apartment for three years with a 10% increase in rent each year, what would be the DIFFERENCE between the total rent he would pay and the rent he would have paid had he chosen the three-year lease?

   A. $266.64   B. $276.64   C. $1,425.60   D. $1,692.24

8. A certain task that an assistant performs takes approximately 45 minutes per unit of work. Seventy-five percent of his work day is spent on this task.
   Assuming that he works seven hours per day, how many work days will it take him to finish 1,470 units of work?

   A. 153   B. 210   C. 240   D. 270

9. It takes 5 1/2 gallons of paint to paint an average apartment, and it requires 18 man hours.
   If the price of paint increases $2.40 per gallon and the pay of the painters increases $2.65 per hour, what is the INCREASE in the cost of painting an apartment?

   A. $49.90   B. $50.90   C. $59.90   D. $60.90

10. A government employee can process a certain type of report in 23 minutes.
    How many such reports could he finish processing in a work day from 9:00 A.M. to 5:00 P.M., with a 45-minute lunch break and two 10-minute coffee breaks?

    A. 16   B. 17   C. 18   D. 19

11. The income of a tenant family is as follows: The husband has a gross income of $280 per week; the wife has a gross income of $220 per week. Deductions from gross family income total $116 per week, plus an allowable child care expense of $56 per week.
    What is the net annual income of the family after deductions and allowable child care expenses?

    A. $16,656   B. $17,056   C. $18,656   D. $19,056

12. Assume that you receive the following bills and coins for use as a change fund: 180 twenty-dollar bills, 110 ten-dollar bills, 125 five-dollar bills, 100 one-dollar bills, 200 quarters, 125 dimes, 50 nickels, and 150 pennies. You cash checks for tenants out of this fund in the following amounts: $134.96, $83.84, $76.96, and $74.37.
    The BALANCE in the fund after paying out these amounts should be

    A. $4,096.37   B. $5,021.47   C. $5,121.37   D. $5,233.87

13. Suppose that a tenant has paid a rent of $312.80 per month for six months and the rent is then increased by 5%.
    After paying the increased rent for six months, how much MORE money has the tenant paid in rent than was paid in the previous six months?

    A. $15.64   B. $93.84   C. $112.56   D. $187.68

14. Assume that $13,965.31 was collected at a project on a Monday.
If the collections at this project on Tuesday were 7% more than on Monday, then the Tuesday total was MOST NEARLY

    A. $12,987.74   B. $14,492.90
    C. $14,942.88   D. $14,977.57

15. Suppose that $12,864 was collected on a Thursday and $17,243 was collected on Friday.
The percentage increase in Friday's collections over Thursday's collections was MOST NEARLY

    A. 25%   B. 34%   C. 66%   D. 75%

16. If the total monthly rent roll at Project Y is $116,610 and the cash collections of current rent at the end of the first week of the month totaled 93% of the total monthly rent roll, then the amount of current rent still uncollected was

    A. $7,160.70   B. $8,162.70
    C. $8,273.30   D. $8,621.30

17. A city employee whose weekly pay was $432.60 for a 35-hour work week was required to work 7 hours overtime during one week. The employee asked what the pay rate was for this overtime and was informed that the first five hours would be paid at his regular hourly rate and the next two hours at one and one-half times his regular rate.
According to this information, the total amount of pay for overtime worked by this employee during this week was

    A. $61.80   B. $86.52   C. $98.88   D. $136.68

18. If 3/4 of a number is 10 more than 1/2 the number, the number is

    A. 8   B. 20   C. 40   D. 50

19. Instead of dividing a number by 5, you can achieve the same result by

    A. multiplying by 1/2   B. dividing by 1/2
    C. multiplying by .2   D. dividing by .2

20. What percent of 4/5 is 7/10?

    A. 56%   B. 87 1/2%   C. 114 2/7%   D. 178 4/7%

21. When a number is multiplied by three and then divided by 1/4, the net result is that the number is

    A. multiplied by 3/4   B. multiplied by 4/3
    C. multiplied by 12   D. divided by 12

22. Three tellers, all working at the same rate of speed, were able to post 1,260 rent charges in 14 hours.
How long would the job have taken if only two of these tellers had been assigned? _____ hours.

    A. 7   B. 9 1/3   C. 18   D. 21

23. A teller filed 440 ledger cards in an hour. If this amounted to 12 1/2% of the task, what was the TOTAL number of cards he was required to file?

    A. 360   B. 3,520   C. 3,600   D. 5,402

24. $5,470.80 is to be paid to 47 employees, each of whom will receive the same amount in cash.
If in making the payment you give each employee the minimum number of bills and coins possible, how many $1 bills will you need to meet the payroll?

    A. 47   B. 94   C. 188   D. 282

25. A commercial tenant pays an annual rental under a graduated percentage lease. The annual rental is based on gross sales for the year and is computed as follows:

    On the first $50,000 of gross sales   - 5%
    On the next $25,000   - 4 1/2%
    On the next $15,000   - 3 1/2%
    On the next $10,000   - 2 1/2%
    On sales in excess of $100,000   - 1 1/4%

His gross sales for the year were $116,292.80.
His rental for that year was MOST NEARLY

    A. $2,703.60   B. $4,603.60
    C. $5,203.60   D. $11,453.60

KEY (CORRECT ANSWERS)

1. C		11. B	
2. C		12. C	
3. B		13. B	
4. A		14. C	
5. C		15. B	
6. A		16. B	
7. A		17. C	
8. B		18. C	
9. D		19. C	
10. C		20. B	

21. C
22. D
23. B
24. A
25. B

SOLUTIONS TO PROBLEMS

1. Using a horizontal dotted line, we construct two rectangles. Total area = (270')(70') + (115')(150'-70') = 28,100 sq.ft.

2. (30')(50')(2/3') = 1000 cu.ft., which contains (1000)(7.5) = 7500 gallons. Then, 7500 ÷ 30 = 250 minutes

3. 20,000 ÷ 900 = 22.$\bar{2}$ man-hours. To complete the job in 4 hours, use 22.2 ÷ 4 ≈ 6 cleaners.

4. (35')(45') = 1575 sq.ft. Then, 1575 ÷ 9 = 175 sq.yds.

5. ($468)(2) - $284 = $652 net income. With changes, ($484)(2) -$320 = $648 new net income. Monthly net income = $4

6. ($484)(2) - ($468)(2) = $32. Then, $32 + $36 = $68. Finally, $544 ⊤ $68 = 8 months.

7.
    ```
    Yr. 1: $242 x 12 =            2904.00
    Yr. 2: + 10% + $290.40 =      3194.40
    Yr. 3: + 10% + $310.44 =      3573.84
                                  9612.24
    9612.24  9612.24 - 9345.60 = $266.64
    ```

8. (.75)(7) = 5.25 hrs. assigned to this task per day. 1470 units of work will require (1470)(45) = 66,150 min. Since he has 5.25 hours = 315 min. each day, the number of days needed = 66,150 ÷ 315 = 210.

9. Change in cost = ($2.40)(5.5) + ($2.65)(18) = $60.90

10. From 9:00 AM to 5:00 PM is 8 hours. Then, 480 - 45 - (2)(10) = 415 min. Finally, 415 ÷ 23 = 18

11. $280 + $220 - $116 - $56 = $328. Then, ($328)(52) = $17,056 annually.

12. (180)($20) + (110)($10) + (125)($5) + (100)($1) + (200)($0.25) + (125)($0.10) + (50)($0.05) + (150)($0.01) - $134.96 - $83.84 - $76.96 - $74.37 = $5121.37

13. ($312.80)(6) = $1876.80. With the 5% increase, (312.80)(1.05)(6) = $1970.64. The additional cost = $93.84

14. ($13,965.31)(1.07) = $14,942.88

15. $17,243 - $12,864 = $4379. Then, $\dfrac{\$4379}{\$12,864} \approx 34\%$

16. Amount uncollected = (.07)($116,610) = $8162.70

17. $432.60 ÷ 35 = $12.36 per hour on regular pay. His overtime pay per hour = ($12.36)(1.5) = $18.54. His pay for extra time = (5)($12.36) + (2)($18.54) = $98.88.

6 (#2)

18. Let x = missing number. Then, 3/4 x = 10 + 1/2 x. Simplifying, 1/4 x = 10. Solving, x = 40

19. Dividing by 5 is equivalent to multiplying by 1/5 = .2

20. $\dfrac{7}{10} \div \dfrac{4}{5} = \dfrac{7}{10} \cdot \dfrac{5}{4} = \dfrac{7}{8} = 87.5\%$

21. Since dividing by 1/4 means multiplying by 4, the net result for the given statement is multiplying by (3)(4) = 12

22. (3)(14) = 42 worker-hours. Then, 42 ÷ 2 = 21 hours

23. 440 ÷ .125 = 3520 ledger cards

24. $5470.80 ÷ 47 = $116.40. By using the minimum number of bills, each employee would receive one $1 bill toward the $116.40. Thus, for 47 employees, 47 $1 bills would be needed.

25. Total rental - (.05)($50,000) + (.045)($25,000) + (.035)($15,000) + (.025)($10,000) + (.0125X16,292.80) = $4603.66 ≈ $4603.60

TEST 3

DIRECTIONS: Each question or incomplete statement is followed by several suggested answers or completions. Select the one that BEST answers the question or completes the statement. *PRINT THE LETTER OF THE CORRECT ANSWER IN THE SPACE AT THE RIGHT.*

1. 1/6 is the same as 1.____
   A. .16 2/3%   B. 16 2/3%   C. .165   D. 16 2/3

2. 205% written as a decimal is 2.____
   A. .0205   B. .205   C. 2.05   D. 20.5

3. The sum of the fractions 2/3, 2/4, 5/6, and 7/8 is 3.____
   A. 1 15/16   B. 2 1/4   C. 2 3/4   D. 2 7/8

4. 24 3/8 multiplied by 48 amounts to 4.____
   A. 1,115   B. 1,121   C. 1,160   D. 1,170

5. One hundred pennies weigh 15 oz. 5.____
   The value of 4 lbs., 5 oz. of pennies is
   A. $4.33   B. $4.50   C. $4.60   D. $5.13

6. Which of the following is GREATER than .5? 6.____
   A. 1/8   B. 5/9   C. 5.5%   D. 20%

7. A recreation leader and his assistant arranged a picnic in the country for a group of 20 project tenants. Five tenants went in the leader's car and five went in the assistant's car, each tenant paying his driver $1.30 for the roundtrip. The ten tenants who went by bus paid $2.50 for the roundtrip. It was agreed that the tenants who went by car would each pay an additional amount which would be distributed to the tenants who went by bus so that all the tenants would pay the same amount for transportation.
   What ADDITIONAL amount would a tenant who went by car pay? 7.____
   A. 60¢   B. 70¢   C. 90¢   D. $1.20

8. An employee whose normal work day was 7 hours was required to work overtime, for which he took compensatory time off on an hour-for-hour basis in lieu of overtime pay. In a month with 21 working days, he worked as follows: 8.____
   First week - worked overtime 5 1/2 hours and took off 4 1/4 hours
   Second week - worked overtime 10 hours and took off 10 1/2 hours
   Third week - took one vacation day
   Balance of month - worked regular schedule
   How many hours did he work during the month?
   A. 129 3/4   B. 135 1/4   C. 139 3/4   D. 140 3/4

9. Suppose that you have received the following bills and coins for use as a change fund: 230 twenty-dollar bills, 130 ten-dollar bills, 175 five-dollar bills, 150 one-dollar bills, 220 quarters, 150 dimes, 60 nickels, and 200 pennies. You cash checks for tenants out of this fund in the following amounts: $120.75, $95.57, $75.40, and $48.50.
The balance of cash in the fund after paying out these amounts SHOULD be

   A. $5,159.88   B. $5,659.78   C. $6,649.88   D. $6,659.78

10. A caretaker received $350 for having worked from Monday through Friday, 9 A.M. to 5 P.M. with one hour a day for lunch.
The number of hours the caretaker would have to work to earn $60 is

   A. 10
   B. 6
   C. 70 divided by 12
   D. 70 minus 12

11. If the cost of a broom went up from $8.00 to $12.00, the percent INCREASE in the original cost is

   A. A. 20   B. 25   C. 33 1/3   D. 50

12. The AVERAGE of the numbers 3, 5, 7, 8, 12 is

   A. 5   B. 6   C. 7   D. 8

13. The cost of 100 bags of cotton cleaning cloths, 89 pounds per bag, at 70 cents per pound, is

   A. $5,493.50   B. $6,230.00   C. $7,000.00   D. $8,900.00

14. If 5 1/2 bags of sweeping compound cost $55.00, then 6 1/2 bags would cost

   A. $60.00   B. $62.50   C. $65.00   D. $67.50

15. The cost of cleaning supplies in a project averaged $3,300 a month during the first 8 months of the year.
How much can be spent each month for the last four months if the total amount that can be spent for cleaning supplies for the year is $38,800?

   A. $1,240   B. $2,200   C. $3,100   D. $3,300

16. A shelf in a supply closet can safely hold only 100 pounds. A package of paper towels weighs 2 pounds, a carton of disinfectant weighs 8 pounds, and a box of soap weighs 1 pound. There are already 6 cartons of disinfectant and 6 boxes of soap on the shelf.
How many packages of towels can be SAFELY placed there?

   A. 20   B. 23   C. 25   D. 27

17. A cleaning solution is made up of 4 gallons of water, 1 pint of liquid soap, and 1 pint of ammonia.
How many gallons of water are needed to use up a gallon of ammonia?
_____ gallons.

   A. 8   B. 16   C. 24   D. 32

18. Suppose a caretaker has 50 stair halls to clean.
If he cleans 74% of them, the number of stair halls still UNCLEANED is

   A. 38   B. 26   C. 24   D. 13

19. If a man has a 12-foot piece of wood and wishes to cut it into two pieces so that one piece is twice as long as the other, the LONGER piece should be _____ feet. 19._____

   A. 7   B. 7 1/2   C. 8   D. 8 1/2

20. A city employee, whose weekly salary is $537.60 for a 35-hour workweek, was required to work 7 hours overtime during one week. The employee asked what the pay rate was for this overtime and was informed that he would be paid for the first five hours at his regular hourly rate and the next two hours at one and one-half times his regular hourly rate. According to this information, the GROSS pay for overtime worked by this employee during this week was 20._____

   A. $76.80   B. $107.52   C. $122.88   D. $161.28

21. Assume that you receive the following bills and coins for use as a change fund: 120 twenty-dollar bills, 150 ten-dollar bills, 100 five-dollar bills, 100 one-dollar bills, 100 quarters, 50 dimes, 25 nickels, and 200 pennies. You cash checks for tenants out of this fund in the following amounts: $189.30, $87.16, $72.90, and $68.50.
The cash balance in the fund after cashing these checks should be 21._____

   A. $4,115.39   B. $4,325.01
   C. $4,713.09   D. $4,951.11

22. If the total monthly rent roll at Project X is $121,990 and the cash collections of current rent at the end of the first week of the month were 95% of the total monthly rent roll, then the amount of current rent still uncollected was 22._____

   A. $5,679.90   B. $6,099.50
   C. $6,211.90   D. $6,312.50

23. Suppose that a tenant has paid $172.40 per month in rent for six months and the rent is then increased by 5%. After paying the increased rent for six months, how much MORE money has the tenant paid in rent than was paid in the previous six months? 23._____

   A. $8.62   B. $51.72   C. $57.52   D. $60.58

24. The rents for three families in a relocation site come to a total of $9,720 per year. If Family A pays $3,480 per year and Family B pays $2,400 per year, how much does Family C pay? 24._____

   A. $2,760   B. $3,840   C. $4,200   D. $5,800

25. In a certain project, an exterminator is told to spray 120 apartments, 40 apartments, 20 basements, 80 apartments, 50 storerooms, and 10 compactors.
The TOTAL number of apartments which should be sprayed is 25._____

   A. 240   B. 260   C. 310   D. 320

KEY (CORRECT ANSWERS)

1.	B	11.	D
2.	C	12.	C
3.	D	13.	B
4.	D	14.	C
5.	C	15.	C
6.	B	16.	B
7.	A	17.	D
8.	D	18.	D
9.	D	19.	C
10.	B	20.	C

21. A
22. B
23. B
24. B
25. A

5 (#3)

SOLUTIONS TO PROBLEMS

1. $\frac{1}{6} = .1\overline{6} = 16\frac{2}{3}\%$

2. 205% = 2.05

3. 2/3 + 2/4 + 5/6 + 7/8 = 69/24 = 2 7/8

4. (24 3/8)(48) = (24.375)(48) = 1170

5. 4 lbs. 5 oz. = 69 oz. Let x = required weight. Then, $\frac{\$1.00}{15} = \frac{x}{69}$ Solving, x = $4.60

6. $\frac{5}{9} = .\overline{5} > .5$

7. The total paid by all 20 tenants was (10)($1.30) + (10)($2.50) = $38.00. If each person had paid the same amount, it would be $38.00 v 20 = $1.90. So, the additional amount owed by each tenant who went by car was $0.60.

8. 1st week: 35 + 5 1/2 - 4 1/4 = 36 1/4 hrs. 2nd week: 35 + 10 - 10 1/2 = 34 1/2 hrs. 3rd week: (7)(4) = 28 hrs. Balance of month: (7)(21-15) = 42 hrs. Total hrs. = 140 3/4

9. (230)($20) + (130)($10) + (175)($5) + (150)($1) + (220)(.25) + (150)(.10) + (60)(.05) + (200)(.01) - $120.75 - $95.57 - $75.40 - $48.50 = $6659.78

10. 9 AM to 5 PM minus 1 hour for lunch = 35 hrs./wk. x = required number of hrs. Then, $\frac{\$350}{35} = \frac{\$60}{x}$. Solving, x = 6

11. ($12.00-$8.00) ÷ $8.00 = 4 = 50%

12. (3+5+7+8+12) ÷ 5 = 35 ÷ 5 = 7

13. (89)(100) = 8900 lbs. Then, (8900)($0.70) = $6230.00

14. Let x = cost. $\frac{5.5}{\$55} = \frac{6.5}{x}$. Solving, x = $65.00

15. $38,800 - (8)($3300) = $12,400. Then, $12,400 ÷ 4 = $3100

16. (6)(8) + (6)(1) = 54 lbs. Only 100 - 54 = 46 more pounds can be placed on the shelf. Finally, 46 ÷ 2 = 23 pkgs. of towels.

17. Since 8 pints = 1 gallon, a gallon of ammonia requires (8)(4) = 32 gallons of water.

18. (50)(.26) = 13 halls uncleaned

19. Let x = longer piece and 1/2 x = shorter piece. Then, x + 1/2 x = 12 So, 3/2 x = 12, and x = 8 feet

20. $537.60 ÷ 35 = $15.36 per hour for regular pay. Overtime pay per hour = (15.36)(1.5) = $23.04. His overtime pay = (5)($15.36) + (2)($23.04) = $122.88

21. (120)($20) + (150)($10) + (100)($5) + (100)($1) + (100)($0.25) + (50)($0.10) + (25)($0.05) + (200)($0.01) - $189.30 - $87.16 - $72.90 - $68.50 = $4115.39.

22. ($121,990)(.05) = $6099.50 uncollected

23. ($172.40)(1.05) = 181.02. Then, ($181.02)(6) - ($172.40)(6) = $51.72

24. Family C pays $9720 - $3480 - $2400 = $3840

25. 120 + 40 + 80 = 240 apartments

CLERICAL ABILITIES
EXAMINATION SECTION
TEST 1

DIRECTIONS: Each question or incomplete statement is followed by several suggested answers or completions. Select the one that BEST answers the question or completes the statement. *PRINT THE LETTER OF THE CORRECT ANSWER IN THE SPACE AT THE RIGHT.*

Questions 1-4.

DIRECTIONS: Questions 1 through 4 are to be answered on the basis of the information given below.

The most commonly used filing system and the one that is easiest to learn is alphabetical filing. This involves putting records in an A to Z order, according to the letters of the alphabet. The name of a person is filed by using the following order: first, the surname or last name; second, the first name; third, the middle name or middle initial. For example, *Henry C. Young* is filed under *Y* and thereafter under *Young, Henry C.* The name of a company is filed in the same way. For example, *Long Cabinet Co.* is filed under *L* while *John T. Long Cabinet Co.* is filed under *L* and thereafter under *Long, John T. Cabinet Co.*

1. The one of the following which lists the names of persons in the CORRECT alphabetical order is:
   A. Mary Carrie, Helen Carrol, James Carson, John Carter
   B. James Carson, Mary Carrie, John Carter, Helen Carrol
   C. Helen Carrol, James Carson, John Carter, Mary Carrie
   D. John Carter, Helen Carrol, Mary Carrie, James Carson

1._____

2. The one of the following which lists the names of persons in the CORRECT alphabetical order is:
   A. Jones, John C.; Jones, John A.; Jones, John P.; Jones, John K.
   B. Jones, John P.; Jones, John K.; Jones, John C.; Jones, John A.
   C. Jones, John A.; Jones, John C.; Jones, John K.; Jones, John P.
   D. Jones, John K.; Jones, John C.; Jones, John A.; Jones, John P.

2._____

3. The one of the following which lists the names of the companies in the CORRECT alphabetical order is:
   A. Blane Co., Blake Co., Block Co., Blear Co.
   B. Blake Co., Blane Co., Blear Co., Block Co.
   C. Block Co., Blear Co., Blane Co., Blake Co.
   D. Blear Co., Blake Co., Blane Co., Block Co.

3._____

4. You are to return to the file an index card on *Barry C. Wayne Materials and Supplies Co.*
   Of the following, the CORRECT alphabetical group that you should return the index card to is

   A. A to G B. H to M C. N to S D. T to Z

   4.____

Questions 5-10.

DIRECTIONS: In each of Questions 5 through 10, the names of four people are given. For each question, choose as your answer the one of the four names given which should be filed FIRST according to the usual system of alphabetical filing of names, as described in the following paragraph.

In filing names, you must start with the last name. Names are filed in order of the first letter of the last name, then the second letter, etc. Therefore, BAILY would be filed before BROWN, which would be filed before COLT. A name with fewer letters of the same type comes first, i.e., Smith before Smithe. If the last names are the same, the names are filed alphabetically by the first name. If the first name is an initial, a name with an initial would come before a first name that starts with the same letter as the initial. Therefore, I. BROWN would come before IRA BROWN. Finally, if both last name and first name are the same, the name would be filed alphabetically by the middle name, once again an initial coming before a middle name which starts with the same letter as the initial. If there is no middle name at all, the name would come before those with middle initials or names.

SAMPLE QUESTION: A. Lester Daniels
B. William Dancer
C. Nathan Danzig
D. Dan Lester

The last names beginning with D are filed before the last name beginning with L. Since DANIELS, DANCER, and DANZIG all begin with the same three letters, you must look at the fourth letter of the last name to determine which name should be filed first. C comes before I or Z in the alphabet, so DANCER is filed before DANIELS or DANZIG. Therefore, the answer to the above sample question is B.

5. A. Scott Biala
   B. Mary Byala
   C. Martin Baylor
   D. Francis Bauer

   5.____

6. A. Howard J. Black
   B. Howard Black
   C. J. Howard Black
   D. John H. Black

   6.____

7. A. Theodora Garth Kingston
   B. Theadore Barth Kingston
   C. Thomas Kingston
   D. Thomas T. Kingston

   7.____

8. A. Paulette Mary Huerta
    B. Paul M. Huerta
    C. Paulette L. Huerta
    D. Peter A. Huerta

9. A. Martha Hunt Morgan
    B. Martin Hunt Morgan
    C. Mary H. Morgan
    D. Martine H. Morgan

10. A. James T. Meerschaum
    B. James M. Mershum
    C. James F. Mearshaum
    D. James N. Meshum

Questions 11-14.

DIRECTIONS: Questions 11 through 14 are to be answered SOLELY on the basis of the following information.

You are required to file various documents in file drawers which are labeled according to the following pattern:

DOCUMENTS

MEMOS		LETTERS	
File	Subject	File	Subject
84PM1	(A-L)	84PC1	(A-L)
84PM2	(M-Z)	84PC2	(M-Z)

REPORTS		INQUIRIES	
File	Subject	File	Subject
84PR1	(A-L)	84PQ1	(A-L)
84PR2	(M-Z)	84PQ2	(M-Z)

11. A letter dealing with a burglary should be filed in the drawer labeled
    A. 84PM1   B. 84PC1   C. 84PR1   D. 84PQ2

12. A report on Statistics should be found in the drawer labeled
    A. 84PM1   B. 84PC2   C. 84PR2   D. 84PQS

13. An inquiry is received about parade permit procedures. It should be filed in the drawer labeled
    A. 84PM2   B. 84PC1   C. 84PR1   D. 84PQ2

14. A police officer has a question about a robbery report you filed. You should pull this file from the drawer labeled
    A. 84PM1   B. 84PM2   C. 84PR1   D. 84PR2

4 (#1)

Questions 15-22.

DIRECTIONS: Each of Questions 15 through 22 consists of four or six numbered names. For each question, choose the option (A, B, C, or D) which indicates the order in which the names should be filed in accordance with the following filing instructions:
- File alphabetically according to last name, then first name, then middle initial.
- File according to each successive letter within a name.
- When comparing two names in which the letters in the longer name are identical to the corresponding letters in the shorter name, the shorter name is filed first.
- When the last names are the same, initials are always filed before names beginning with the same letter.

15. I.   Ralph Robinson
     II. Alfred Ross
     III. Luis Robles
     IV. James Roberts

The CORRECT filing sequence for the above names should be
A. IV, II, I, III   B. I, IV, III, II   C. III, IV, I, II   D. IV, I, III, II

15.____

16. I.   Irwin Goodwin
     II. Inez Gonzalez
     III. Irene Goodman
     IV. Ira S. Goodwin
     V.   Ruth I. Goldstein
     VI. M.B. Goodman

The CORRECT filing sequence for the above names should be
A. V, II, I, IV, III, VI   B. V, II, VI, III, IV, I
C. V, II, III, VI, IV, I   D. V, II, III, VI, I, IV

16.____

17. I.   George Allan
     II. Gregory Allen
     III. Gary Allen
     IV. George Allen

The CORRECT filing sequence for the above names should be
A. IV, III, I, II   B. I, IV, II, III   C. III, IV, I, II   D. I, III, IV, II

17.____

128

5 (#1)

18. I. Simon Kauffman
    II. Leo Kaufman
    III. Robert Kaufmann
    IV. Paul Kauffmann

    The CORRECT filing sequence for the above names should be
    A. I, IV, II, III   B. II, IV, III, I   C. III, II, IV, I   D. I, II, III, IV

    18._____

19. I. Roberta Williams
    II. Robin Wilson
    III. Roberta Wilson
    IV. Robin Williams

    The CORRECT filing sequence for the above names should be
    A. III, II, IV, I   B. I, IV, III, II   C. I, II, III, IV   D. III, I, II, IV

    19._____

20. I. Lawrence Shultz
    II. Albert Schultz
    III. Theodore Schwartz
    IV. Thomas Schwarz
    V. Alvin Schultz
    VI. Leonard Shultz

    The CORRECT filing sequence for the above names should be
    A. II, V, III, IV, I, VI   B. IV, III, V, I, II, VI
    C. II, V, I, VI, III, IV   D. I, VI, II, V, III, IV

    20._____

21. I. McArdle
    II. Mayer
    III. Maletz
    IV. McNiff
    V. Meyer
    VI. MacMahon

    The CORRECT filing sequence for the above names should be
    A. I, IV, VI, III, II, V   B. II, I, IV, VI, III, V
    C. VI, III, II, I, IV, V   D. VI, III, II, V, I, IV

    21._____

22. I. Jack E. Johnson
    II. R.H. Jackson
    III. Bertha Jackson
    IV. J.T. Johnson
    V. Ann Johns
    VI. John Jacobs

    The CORRECT filing sequence for the above names should be
    A. II, III, VI, V, IV, I   B. III, II, VI, V, IV, I
    C. VI, II, III, I, V, IV   D. III, II, VI, IV, V, I

    22._____

Questions 23-30.

DIRECTIONS: The code table below shows 10 letters with matching numbers. For each question, there are three sets of letters. Each set of letters is followed by a set of numbers which may or may not match their correct letter according to the code table. For each question, check all three sets of letters and numbers and mark your answer:
    A. if no pairs are correctly matched
    B. if only one pair is correctly matched
    C. if only two pairs are correctly matched
    D. if all three pairs are correctly matched

CODE TABLE

T	M	V	D	S	P	R	G	B	H
1	2	3	4	5	6	7	8	9	0

SAMPLE QUESTION: TMVDSP – 123456
                                  RGBHTM – 789011
                                  DSPRGB – 256789

    In the sample question above, the first set of numbers correctly match its set of letters. But the second and third pairs contain mistakes. In the second pair, M is correctly matched with number 1. According to the code table, letter M should be correctly matched with number 2. In the third pair, the letter D is incorrectly matched with number 2. According to the code table, letter D should be correctly matched with number 4. Since only one of the pairs is correctly matched, the answer to this sample question is B.

23.   RSBMRM – 759262   23.____
        GDSRVH – 845730
        VDBRTM - 349713

24.   TGVSDR – 183247   24.____
        SMHRDP – 520647
        TRMHSR - 172057

25.   DSPRGM – 456782   25.____
        MVDBHT – 234902
        HPMDBT - 062491

26.   BVPTRD – 936184   26.____
        GDPHMB – 807029
        GMRHMV - 827032

27.   MGVRSH – 283750   27.____
        TRDMBS – 174295
        SPRMGV - 567283

28. SGBSDM – 489542
    MGHPTM – 290612
    MPBMHT - 269301

    28.____

29. TDPBHM – 146902
    VPBMRS – 369275
    GDMBHM - 842902

    29.____

30. MVPTBV – 236194
    PDRTMB – 47128
    BGTMSM - 981232

    30.____

KEY (CORRECT ANSWERS)

1.	A	11.	B	21.	C
2.	C	12.	C	22.	B
3.	B	13.	D	23.	B
4.	D	14.	D	24.	B
5.	D	15.	D	25.	C
6.	B	16.	C	26.	A
7.	B	17.	D	27.	D
8.	B	18.	A	28.	A
9.	A	19.	B	29.	D
10.	C	20.	A	30.	A

TEST 2

DIRECTIONS: Each question or incomplete statement is followed by several suggested answers or completions. Select the one that BEST answers the question or completes the statement. *PRINT THE LETTER OF THE CORRECT ANSWER IN THE SPACE AT THE RIGHT.*

Questions 1-10.

DIRECTIONS: Questions 1 through 10 each consists of two columns, each containing four lines of names, numbers and/or addresses. For each question, compare the lines in Column I with the lines in Column II to see if they match exactly, and mark your answer A, B, C, or D, according to the following instructions:
    A. all four lines match exactly
    B. only three lines match exactly
    C. only two lines match exactly
    D. only one line matches exactly

<u>COLUMN I</u>   <u>COLUMN II</u>

1.   I.   Earl Hodgson   Earl Hodgson   1.____
      II.   1409870   1408970
      III.   Shore Ave.   Schore Ave.
      IV.   Macon Rd.   Macon Rd.

2.   I.   9671485   9671485   2.____
      II.   470 Astor Court   470 Astor Court
      III.   Halprin, Phillip   Halperin, Phillip
      IV.   Frank D. Poliseo   Frank D. Poliseo

3.   I.   Tandem Associates   Tandom Associates   3.____
      II.   144-17 Northern Blvd.   144-17 Northern Blvd.
      III.   Alberta Forchi   Albert Forchi
      IV.   Kings Park, NY 10751   Kings Point, NY 10751

4.   I.   Bertha C. McCormack   Bertha C. McCormack   4.____
      II.   Clayton, MO   Clayton, MO
      III.   976-4242   976-4242
      IV.   New City, NY 10951   New City, NY 10951

5.   I.   George C. Morill   George C. Morrill   5.____
      II.   Columbia, SC 29201   Columbia, SD 29201
      III.   Louis Ingham   Louis Ingham
      IV.   3406 Forest Ave.   3406 Forest Ave.

6.   I.   506 S. Elliott Pl.   506 S. Elliott Pl.   6.____
      II.   Herbert Hall   Hurbert Hall
      III.   4712 Rockaway Pkway   4712 Rockaway Pkway
      IV.   169 E. 7 St.   169 E. 7 St.

2 (#2)

7. I.   345 Park Ave.   345 Park Pl.   7._____
    II. Colman Oven Corp.   Coleman Oven Corp.
    III. Robert Conte   Robert Conti
    IV. 6179846   6179846

8. I.   Grigori Schierber   Grigori Schierber   8._____
    II. Des Moines, Iowa   Des Moines, Iowa
    III. Gouverneur Hospital   Gouverneur Hospital
    IV. 91-35 Cresskill Pl.   91-35 Cresskill Pl.

9. I.   Jeffery Janssen   Jeffrey Janssen   9._____
    II. 8041071   8041071
    III. 40 Rockefeller Plaza   40 Rockafeller Plaza
    IV. 407 6 St.   406 7 St.

10. I.   5971996   5871996   10._____
    II. 3113 Knickerbocker Ave.   31123 Knickerbocker Ave.
    III. 8434 Boston Post Rd.   8424 Boston Post Rd.
    IV. Penn Station   Penn Station

Questions 11-14.

DIRECTIONS: Questions 11 through 14 are to be answered by looking at the four groups of names and addresses listed below (I, II, III, and IV), and then finding out the number of groups that have their corresponding numbered lies exactly the same.

         GROUP I   GROUP II
Line 1. Richmond General Hospital   Richman General Hospital
Line 2. Geriatric Clinic   Geriatric Clinic
Line 3. 3975 Paerdegat St.   3975 Peardegat St.
Line 4. Loudonville, New York 11538   Londonville, New York 11538

         GROUP III   GROUP IV
Line 1. Richmond General Hospital   Richmend General Hospital
Line 2. Geriatric Clinic   Geriatric Clinic
Line 3. 3795 Paerdegat St.   3975 Paerdegat St.
Line 4. Loudonville, New York 11358   Loudonville, New York 11538

1. In how many groups is line one exactly the same?   11._____
    A. Two   B. Three   C. Four   D. None

12. In how many groups is line two exactly the same?   12._____
    A. Two   B. Three   C. Four   D. None

13. In how many groups is line three exactly the same?   13._____
    A. Two   B. Three   C. Four   D. None

3 (#2)

14. In how many groups is line four exactly the same?   14._____
    A. Two   B. Three   C. Four   D. None

Questions 15-18.

DIRECTIONS: Each of Questions 15 through 18 has two lists of names and addresses. Each list contains three sets of names and addresses. Check each of the three sets in the list on the right to see if they are the same as the corresponding set in the list on the left. Mark your answers:
   A. if none of the sets in the right list are the same as those in the left list
   B. if only one of the sets in the right list is the same as those in the left list
   C. if only two of the sets in the right list are the same as those in the left list
   D. if all three sets in the right list are the same as those in the left list

15. Mary T. Berlinger   Mary T. Berlinger   15._____
     2351 Hampton St.   2351 Hampton St.
     Monsey, N.Y. 20117   Monsey, N.Y. 20117

     Eduardo Benes   Eduardo Benes
     483 Kingston Avenue   473 Kingston Avenue
     Central Islip, N.Y. 11734   Central Islip, N.Y. 11734

     Alan Carrington Fuchs   Alan Carrington Fuchs
     17 Gnarled Hollow Road   17 Gnarled Hollow Road
     Los Angeles, CA 91635   Los Angeles, CA 91685

16. David John Jacobson   David John Jacobson   16._____
     178 34 St. Apt. 4C   178 53 St. Apt. 4C
     New York, N.Y. 00927   New York, N.Y. 00927

     Ann-Marie Calonella   Ann-Marie Calonella
     7243 South Ridge Blvd.   7243 South Ridge Blvd.
     Bakersfield, CA 96714   Bakersfield, CA 96714

     Pauline M. Thompson   Pauline M. Thomson
     872 Linden Ave.   872 Linden Ave.
     Houston, Texas 70321   Houston, Texas 70321

17. Chester LeRoy Masterton   Chester LeRoy Masterson   17._____
     152 Lacy Rd.   152 Lacy Rd.
     Kankakee, Ill. 54532   Kankakee, Ill. 54532

     William Maloney   William Maloney
     S. LaCrosse Pla.   S. LaCross Pla.
     Wausau, Wisconsin 52136   Wausau, Wisconsin 52146

     Cynthia V. Barnes   Cynthia V. Barnes
     16 Pines Rd.   16 Pines Rd.
     Greenpoint, Miss. 20376   Greenpoint,, Miss. 20376

4 (#2)

18. Marcel Jean Frontenac
    8 Burton On The Water
    Calender, Me. 01471

    J. Scott Marsden
    174 S. Tipton St.
    Cleveland, Ohio

    Lawrence T. Haney
    171 McDonough St.
    Decatur, Ga. 31304

    Marcel Jean Frontenac
    6 Burton On The Water
    Calender, Me. 01471

    J. Scott Marsden
    174 Tipton St.
    Cleveland, Ohio

    Lawrence T. Haney
    171 McDonough St.
    Decatur, Ga. 31304

18.____

Questions 19-26.

DIRECTIONS: Each of Questions 19 through 26 has two lists of numbers. Each list contains three sets of numbers. Check each of the three sets in the list on the right to see if they are the same as the corresponding set in the list on the left. Mark your answers:
- A. if none of the sets in the right list are the same as those in the left list
- B. if only one of the sets in the right list is the same as those in the left list
- C. if only two of the sets in the right list are the same as those in the left list
- D. if all three sets in the right list are the same as those in the left lists

19. 7354183476
    4474747744
    5791430231

    7354983476
    4474747774
    57914302311

19.____

20. 7143592185
    8344517699
    9178531263

    7143892185
    8344518699
    9178531263

20.____

21. 2572114731
    8806835476
    8255831246

    257214731
    8806835476
    8255831246

21.____

22. 331476853821
    6976658532996
    3766042113715

    331476858621
    6976655832996
    3766042113745

22.____

23. 8806663315
    74477138449
    211756663666

    88066633115
    74477138449
    211756663666

23.____

24. 990006966996   99000696996   24.____
    53022219743   53022219843
    4171171117717   4171171177717

25. 24400222433004   24400222433004   25.____
    5300030055000355   5300030055500355
    20000075532002022   20000075532002022

26. 6111666406600011116 6111666406600011116 26.____
    7111300117001100733 7111300117001100733
    26666446664476518   26666446664476518

Questions 27-30.

DIRECTIONS: Questions 27 through 30 are to be answered by picking the answer which is in the correct numerical order, from the lowest number to the highest number, in each question.

27. A. 44533, 44518, 44516, 44547   27.____
    B. 44516, 44518, 44533, 44547
    C. 44547, 44533, 44518, 44516
    D. 44518, 44516, 44547, 44533

28. A. 95587, 95593, 95601, 95620   28.____
    B. 95601, 95620, 95587, 95593
    C. 95593, 95587, 95601. 95620
    D. 95620, 95601, 95593, 95587

29. A. 232212, 232208, 232232, 232223 29.____
    B. 232208, 232223, 232212, 232232
    C. 232208, 232212, 232223, 232232
    D. 232223, 232232, 232208, 232208

30. A. 113419, 113521, 113462, 113462 30.____
    B. 113588, 113462, 113521, 113419
    C. 113521, 113588, 113419, 113462
    D. 113419, 113462, 113521, 113588

KEY (CORRECT ANSWERS)

1. C	11. A	21. C
2. B	12. C	22. A
3. D	13. A	23. D
4. A	14. A	24. A
5. C	15. C	25. C
6. B	16. B	26. C
7. D	17. B	27. B
8. A	18. B	28. A
9. D	19. B	29. C
10. C	20. B	30. D

EXAMINATION SECTION
TEST 1

DIRECTIONS: Each of Questions 1 through 15 consists of a passage which contains one word that is incorrectly used because it is not in keeping with the meaning that the passage is evidently intended to convey. Determine which word is incorrectly used. Then select from the words lettered A, B, C, or D the word which, when substituted for the incorrectly used word, would BEST help to convey the meaning of the passage.

1. A manager must often operate systems that are quite complex, but these systems are an effective vehicle for management. Each system has an input, a process, and an output, and is a self-contained unit, but it is also related to a system of a wider and higher order as well as to its own sub-systems that represent the integration of several systems of the lower order. Thinking in terms of systems restricts his understanding of the multitudinous activities with which he must work, and it also enables him to see better the nature of the complex problems that he faces.

    A. isolation
    B. simplifies
    C. perpetuating
    D. constrains

2. Planning involves, first, the conceiving of goals and the development of alternative courses of future action to achieve the goals. Second, it involves the reduction of these alternatives from a very large number to a small number and finally to one approved course of action, the program. Budgeting probably plays a slight part in the first phase but an increasingly important and decisive part in the second. It facilitates the choice-making process by providing a basis for systematic comparisons among alternatives which take into account their total impacts on both the debit and the credit sides. It thus encourages, and provides some of the tools for, an increasing degree of precision in the planning process. Budgeting is the ingredient of planning which precedes the entire process.

    A. achievement
    B. improved
    C. immediate
    D. disciplines

3. In every instance the burden of proving each of the charges against the employee, which constitute the claimed misconduct or incompetence, must be upon the agency alleging the same. This simply means that it is incumbent upon the agency to establish each of the charges by a fair preponderance of the entire evidence. Unless the Hearing Officer is satisfied that the evidence has fairly and reasonably established the facts asserted by the agency, the agency has not sustained the burden of proof. The Hearing Officer must determine the admissibility of evidence where there is an objection to a question. Although at disciplinary hearings the presentation of the testimony is not limited by strict and technical rules of evidence as in a court, nevertheless the Hearing Officer should at all times consider its relevance and materiality, and then make his determination on the basis of fairness.

    A. corroborate
    B. incredible
    C. disinterested
    D. obligatory

4. The examination of alternative means available for the accomplishment of a given program must proceed along lines somewhat different from the review of alternative programs. In the former, the budget officer should possess sufficient knowledge of operations, and of methods and procedures, to be able to challenge badly conceived projects and to ask the kinds of questions which call forth the orderly processes of administration. This is where budget review and organization and method analysis tend to conflict, and it is here that the reviewing officer who has had operating experience can be most effective in questioning and criticizing management techniques.

   A. personnel
   B. problems
   C. public
   D. merge

5. The employee is not required to submit a written answer to the charges of incompetency or misconduct. The fact that an employee does not choose to submit a written answer should not be taken to mean that he admits guilt. However, the answer provides a means for the accused employee, in writing and for the record, to plead guilty or not guilty to the various charges and specifications, to allege matters tending to disprove the charges, including his good character and reputation, to allege any incriminating circumstances and also to plead a favorable record of service and conduct which might tend to lessen the penalty. Upon receipt of the employee's written answer to the charges, the answer should be carefully analyzed and any allegations therein verified. It may also be necessary to gather new evidence for the hearing in relation to allegations contained in the answer.

   A. confidential
   B. mitigative
   C. particularize
   D. procedural

6. In an article in the Harvard Business Review ("Human Relations or Human Resources"), Raymond E. Miles expounded a human resources theory of management. He declared that a manager's job cannot be viewed as merely one of giving direction and obtaining cooperation; rather, it is one of creating an environment in which the total resources of his department can be utilized. In this environment, the manager shares information and modifies departmental decisions with his employees and encourages their self-direction, not to improve their role satisfactions but to improve the decision making and the total performance efficiency of the organization. Many decisions are made more efficiently by those directly involved in and affected by them. In fact, Miles added, the more important the decisions, the greater the manager's obligation to encourage subordinate self-direction.

   A. actuate
   B. appearance
   C. compulsion
   D. discusses

7. Each organization follows a particular philosophy of management selected from a spectrum ranging from authoritarian to participative. If it adopts an approach in which the manager makes all the decisions and passes them on to subordinates for consideration, it follows an authoritarian philosophy that determines its organization structure and climate. Its structure will follow closely the pattern of many levels of management, tight spans of control, and formal channels of communication. The direction of information flow will be downward, supervisors will have little trust in subordinates, and a high degree of emphasis will be placed on management controls.

   A. approve
   B. concentrated
   C. discretionary
   D. execution

8. Besides the ability to comprehend the magnitude of decisions the ability to deal with decision complexity also differs from person to person. Most human beings are discouraged only with a two-option decision, seeing reality in terms of black or white and hardly ever noticing the gray. Even when there is a choice of three or four pretty well-defined options, a human being will consciously or unconsciously reduce them to two. It takes a good deal of training and education plus a highly developed intellectual structure to handle multi-option decisions and to actively seek a third or fourth alternative.

   A. comfortable
   B. enlarging
   C. narrowly
   D. passive

   8._____

9. Manpower planning, like finance; is a management function that cannot be delegated or decentralized. What has often been overlooked in studies of decentralization is that no successful firm has ever decentralized the financial function. Since there has rarely been more than one treasurer in a firm, the centralized, control of finances exercises an auxiliary power over all members in a decentralized organization. Just as the management of financial resources is regularly centralized, so the management of human and, in particular, managerial resources must be centralized and the primary responsibility accepted by the chief executive. In fact, he should consider the direction of the managerial manpower plan to be his top responsibility.

   A. concentration
   B. external
   C. subsidiary
   D. ultimate

   9._____

10. One drawback of the participative-management approach is the lack of solid research to document its contentions. What has been collected is either inconclusive or negative. Laboratory experiments have repeatedly demonstrated that groups that are organized to counter interpersonal comfort, openness, familiarity, and cohesiveness perform poorly. At least one study, in a large insurance company, of different styles of management revealed that while greater acceptance of leadership and high morale were present in the division led by the manager who believes in democratic supervision, this division's performance results were no better than those achieved by the authoritarian leaders.

    A. disputed
    B. emphasise
    C. inconsistency
    D. resistance

    10._____

11. An organization experiences continuous changes which, taken together, tend to follow a course that can be defined and projected as a trend. Thus, after a company has accumulated sufficient historical data, it is fairly simple to project certain manpower trends. For example, to estimate within a fairly close margin the number of managers who will retire, die, resign, or be discharged in the succeeding 12 months is not so difficult. What is much more difficult and should not even be tried is to predict the number of those individuals who will die, retire, or resign. Simply knowing that, according to present trends, the company must replace 23 managers in the next 12 months is a distinct advantage, and knowing within certain confidence limits how many must be replaced within the next five years affords an even greater advantage

    A. handicap
    B. names
    C. terminated
    D. withheld

    11._____

12. To assess another person, one must first obtain an accurate description of him in relation to the task for which he is being considered, But, to describe a person accurately, we must obtain relevant information about him and this is the sensitive area. Precisely what information is relevant to the role he is asked to play? If it is relevant, have we the right to it? Are there not some personal areas that are open for public inspection? These quite difficult questions are made even more difficult by the unfortunate way they have been raised recently by government agencies. The mishandling of inquiries into the personal background of applicants for positions has been so widespread that it has been necessary to pass laws at all levels restricting the amount and the quality of information that an employer may seek to obtain from a job applicant.

    A. disclosure
    B. processing
    C. prohibition
    D. unavailable

13. An organization's goals must be based on an accurate appraisal of its manpower resources, otherwise they will be like the objectives announced by a last-place baseball-team manager in the spring no more than pious hopes set down for their inspirational value. Public officials are quite guilty in this respects establishing targets for full employment, tax reduction, and urban renewal that are totally attainable and hardly within the capacities of those on the payroll. Many businesses follow the same practice, establishing market-penetration or sales goals that are quite beyond the competence and the energy of their employees. Setting goals, therefore, must take into account the probable course of events that is likely to unfold inside and outside the organization. This prediction of future events is known as forecasting.

    A. estimates
    B. laxity
    C. tendency
    D. unrealistic

14. In some organizations, a silent conspiracy can prevail that masks the facts about the managerial situation. Older managers who feel threatened by their advancing age, their creeping obsolescence, or their rapidly changing environment may try to hide their heads in the sands of yesterday. To support themselves, they may try many maneuvers — hiding promising young men, promoting incompetence, or making a farce out of the performance evaluation program. Out of this mass anxiety an "establishment" is born, a highly structured "in" group that invalidates manpower rules designed to insure its own security. This is the system that old men cherish and young men rail a gainst, that blights an organization like a creeping cancer and slowly destroys it as, all the while, its presence remains unfelt until it is fatal.

    A. enforces
    B. erosion
    C. manipulate
    D. terminating

15. Z. Pietrowski found that the successful top executive strives more intensively for personal achievement, sets more difficult work goals for himself, can adapt emotionally to a variety of people, is more original, and has less insecurity and self-doubt. E. Ghiselli found in his study of 287 managers that the effective manager showed less need for job security than did less effective managers. The effective managers showed the strongest desire for self-actualization, for the opportunity to utilize their talents in customary ways. In summary, the studies indicate quite clearly that the successful manager has a total life pattern of successful endeavor.

    A. conspicuously
    B. creative
    C. effacement
    D. ineffectual

KEY (CORRECT ANSWERS)

1. B
2. D
3. A
4. D
5. B

6. D
7. D
8. A
9. D
10. B

11. B
12. D
13. D
14. A
15. B

TEST 2

DIRECTIONS: Each of the following questions consists of a paragraph which contains one word that is incorrectly used because it is not in keeping with the meaning that the paragraph is evidently intended to convey. Determine which word is incorrectly used. Select from the choices lettered A, B, C, and D the word which, when substituted for the incorrectly used work, would BEST help to convey the meaning of the paragraph.

1. Among the Housing Manager's over-all responsibilities in administering a project is the prevention of the development of conditions which might lead to termination of tenancy and eviction of a tenant. Where there appears to be doubt that a tenant is fully aware of his responsibilities and is thus jeopardizing his tenancy, the Housing Manager should acquaint him with these responsibilities. Where a situation involves behavior of a tenant or a member of his family, the Housing Manager should confirm, through discussions and referrals to social agencies, correction of the conditions before they reach a stage where there is no alternative but termination proceedings.

   A. coordinate B. identify
   C. assert   D. attempt

2. There is one almost universal administrative complaint. The budget is inadequate, Now, between adequacy and inadequacy lie all degrees of adequacy. Further, human wants are modest in relation to human resources. From these two facts we may conclude that the fundamental criterion of administrative decision must be a criterion of efficiency (the degree to which the goals have been reached relative to the available resources) rather than a criterion of adequacy (the degree to which its goals have been reached). The task of the administrator is to maximize social values relative to limited resources.

   A. improve   B. simple
   C. limitless D. optimize

3. Leadership is a personality characteristic based to a large extent on the charisma the leader possesses for his followers. Thus his appeal must be to the emotional and the personal life of the group. A manager, on the other hand, has been entrusted with the responsibility of decision making, which has nothing whatsoever to do with leadership. It is not a personal trait, it is a role that is not administrative and based upon the process of choosing a course of action and committing the group's resources to it. The manager's function is to define goals and objectives, to select a course of action to achieve them, and to evaluate realistically the results of that action. There is little charisma in such a role. Leaders depend for their success on personality, a characteristic that has nothing to do with management. Consequently, leadership and management are most appropriately treated as separate phenomena that are effectively handled simultaneously but not necessarily by the same person.

   A. initiates B. limit
   C. purely   D. rational

4. Where it appears that any City employee may be guilty of corruption or wrongdoing, the Department of Investigation should be informed. The agency itself should then conduct the inquiry immediately only if the Department of Investigation so determines. If during an inquiry it appears that the corruption or wrongdoing may be more serious or widespread than originally suspected, the Department of Investigation should be recontacted immediately. In some instances, it may be necessary to hold the disciplinary hearing prior to the criminal proceedings and it is essential that the conduct of the criminal case not be unnecessarily warranted by the department trial. The transcript and all papers should be kept in a secure place and there should be no disclosure or publicity about what transpired without the approval of the Corpora- tion Counsel and the Commissioner of Investigation.

    A. superseded   B. prejudiced
    C. premature   D. concurrently

4.____

5. It is often easy to enumerate reasons why a housing enterprise succeeds or fails. With so many variables that appear to have a make-or-break impact upon the outcome, there is a natural tendency to over-emphasize the importance of the man, particularly the man in charge. Society subscribes to the idea that housing leadership is important, but society doesn't really believe it. Even top housing managers are dubious about the significance of their own roles in the success or failure of a public enterprise. When things go wrong, they tend to blame the system; when things go right, they modestly give credit to "the team." The only way to manage a housing organization effectively is to give managers authority to run it and then hold them strictly accountable for the results. This idea is hardly new to anyone, however rarely it is carried out in practice. But the idea breaks down because we know so little about picking men who have the capacity to manage large housing enterprises.

    A. coalesce   B. disavows
    C. overlook   D. wavering

5.____

6. The technological and social changes that have occurred in American economy during the rise of the Managerial Society have not only required much more highly trained managers, they have created intense competition for these same men from other sectors of the economy: from the government, from education, and from the nonprofit areas. In the decade between 1954 and 1964, the number of employees in the executive classes of the federal government jumped 58 percent. The result is an unprecedented demand for managers that is likely to continue unabated for the next three decades. If we assume that the shortage has been met in the same way as in technical fields, it is probable that a substantial number of managerial positions are filled by people not fully qualified or that the positions have been reinforced by the inclusion of duties incompatible with those of a manager. Since this latter strategy is most commonly employed, it is possible to assert that many managers are managers in name only.

    A. conflicting   B. diluted
    C. eliminate   D. incumbent

6.____

7. There is also a suspicion in some quarters that admin- istrators have a tendency to be imperialistic, that government officials have an inborn desire to spend more of the taxpayers' money, to hire more people, to build more buildings. Sometimes this charge is couched in more gentle terms, it is suggested that administrators tend to overestimate simply to be on the safe side, so that they will be able to retain some leeway in program administration. Again, there is no doubt that these charges and suspicions are justified in particular cases. The overzealous and overambitious are not unknown in our society, or in any society. But it would be difficult to demonstrate that these tendencies are more widespread in government than elsewhere. Very often, what looks like an overweening ambition may turn out to be regressive administration. The government official who seeks to expand his program may do so because he sees the need, because he would like to do *a* better job, because he is close to the beneficiaries of his program operations.

7._____

- A. responsive
- B. fewer
- C. freedom
- D. targets

KEY (CORRECT ANSWERS)

1. D
2. C
3. C
4. B
5. C
6. B
7. A

EXAMINATION SECTION
TEST 1

DIRECTIONS: Each question or incomplete statement is followed by several suggested answers or completions. Select the one that BEST answers the question or completes the statement. *PRINT THE LETTER OF THE CORRECT ANSWER IN THE SPACE AT THE RIGHT.*

1. Assume that a supervisor finds that his employees have become fatigued from doing a very long and repetitious job.
   The one of the following which would be the BEST way to relieve this fatigue is to
   A. assign other work so that the employees can switch to different assignments in the middle of the day
   B. let the employees listen to a radio while they work
   C. break the job down into very small parts so that each employee can concentrate on one simple task
   D. allow the employees to take frequent rest periods

   1.____

2. Assume that one of your subordinates is injured and will be out for at least six weeks.
   Of the following, the BEST way to handle the work normally assigned to this person is to
   A. allow the work to remain uncompleted until the injured person returns, since he is the one who can BEST do this work
   B. divide this work equally among the persons under your supervision who can do this work
   C. do all the work yourself
   D. give the injured person's work to the most efficient member of your staff

   2.____

3. Suppose that another supervisor tells you about a new way to organize some of your unit's work. The idea sounds good to you. However, before you were in this unit, a similar plan was tried and it failed.
   The MOST important thing for you to do FIRST is to
   A. find out why the previous attempt failed
   B. suggest that the other supervisor tell his idea to top management
   C. try the plan to see whether it works
   D. find proof that the plan has worked elsewhere

   3.____

4. One of your subordinates comes to you with a grievance. You discuss it with him so that you may fully understand the problem as he sees it.
   However, since you are uncertain as to the proper answer, you should
   A. tell him that you cannot help him with this problem
   B. tell him that you will have to check further and make an appointment to see him again
   C. send him to see your immediate superior for a solution to the problem
   D. ask him to find out from his co-workers whether this problem has come up before

   4.____

5. A supervisor reprimanded one of his subordinates severely for making a serious error in judgment while performing an assignment for which he had volunteered.
The supervisor's action was
   A. *incorrect*, chiefly because in the future the worker will probably try to avoid taking on responsibility
   B. *correct*, chiefly because this will insure that the worker will not make the same mistake in the future
   C. *correct*, chiefly because the worker should be discouraged from using his own judgment on the job
   D. *incorrect*, chiefly because the reprimand came too late to correct the error that had already been made

6. Of the following, the BEST way for a supervisor to inform all his subordinates of a change in lunch rules is, in MOST cases, to
   A. call a staff meeting
   B. tell each one individually
   C. issue a memorandum
   D. tell one or two employees to pass the word around

7. For a supervisor to assign work giving only general instructions to his subordinate would be advisable when
   A. the supervisor is confident that the worker knows how to do the job
   B. the assignment is a simple one
   C. the subordinate is himself a supervisory employee
   D. errors in the work will not cause serious delay

8. One of the DISADVANTAGES of setting minimum standards of performance for custodial employees is that
   A. such standards eliminate the basis for evaluating employees
   B. the custodial employees may keep their performance at the minimum level
   C. standards are always subject to change
   D. the supervisor may feel that his initiative is being restricted

9. One of your subordinates has been functioning below his usual level. You feel that something of a personal nature may be affecting his work. When you ask him casually whether anything is wrong, he says everything is fine.
As a next step, it would be BEST to
   A. make frequent casual and humorous comments about the poor quality of his work but refrain, at this time, from any serious discussion
   B. warn him that failure to maintain his customary level of performance might result in disciplinary action
   C. express your concern privately and reveal your interest in the reason for his change in work performance
   D. discuss with him the work of another employee, suggesting that the other employee would be a good example to follow

10. Assume you are teaching a new job to one of your subordinates. After you have demonstrated the job, you can BEST maintain the worker's interest by
    A. showing him training films about the job
    B. giving him printed material that explains why the job is important
    C. having him observe other workers do the job
    D. letting him attempt to do the job by himself under supervision

11. *Insubordination is sometimes a protest against inferior or arbitrary leadership.*
    For the supervisor, the MOST basic implication of the above statement is:
    A. Accusations of insubordination are easy to make, but usually difficult to prove.
    B. Insubordination cannot be permitted if an organization wishes to remain effective.
    C. When an employee discusses an order instead of carrying it out, he has not understood it.
    D. When an employee questions an order, review it to make sure it is reasonable.

12. In appraising a subordinate's mistakes, a supervisor should ALWAYS consider the
    A. absolute number of mistakes, without regard to severity
    B. number of mistakes in proportion to the number of decisions made
    C. total number of mistakes made by other, regardless of assignment
    D. number of mistakes which were discovered upon higher review

13. If you are the supervisor of an office in which the work frequently involves lifting heavy boxes, you should instruct your staff in the proper method of lifting to avoid injury.
    In giving these instructions, you should stress that a person lifting heavy objects MUST
    A. keep his feet close together
    B. bend at the waist
    C. keep his back as straight as possible
    D. use his back muscles to straighten up

14. Of the following, the BEST qualified supervisor is one who
    A. knows the basic principles and procedures of all the jobs which he supervises
    B. has detailed working knowledge of all aspects of the job he supervises but knows little about principles of supervision
    C. is able to do exceptionally well at least one of the jobs which he supervises and as some knowledge of the others
    D. knows little or nothing about most of the jobs which he supervises but knows the principles of supervision

15. The rate at which an employee will learn will vary according to a number of considerations.
    Of the following, which is LEAST likely to be controllable by the supervisor or the trainer? The
    A. manner in which the material is presented
    B. state of readiness of the learner
    C. scheduling of practice sessions
    D. nature of the material

16. When considering whether to use written material rather than oral instructions as a means of giving instructions to employees, the one of the following which should be given GREATEST consideration is the employees'
    A. personal preferences
    B. attitude toward supervision
    C. general educational level
    D. salary level

17. Assume that one of your subordinates has been assigned to attend job training classes.
    The one of the following which would probably be the BEST evidence of the success of the course is that the employee
    A. feels that he has learned something
    B. continues to study after the course is over
    C. has had a good class record
    D. improves in his work performance

18. Of the following, the situation LEAST likely to result if a supervisor shows favoritism toward particular employees is
    A. laxity in the work of the favored employees
    B. resentment from the other, less-favored employees
    C. increased ability among the favored employees
    D. lowering of morale among employees

19. The one of the following reasons for evaluating employees' performance, whether done formally or informally, which is NOT considered to be POSITIVE in nature is to
    A. give individual counsel to employees
    B. motivate employees toward improvement
    C. provide recognition of superior service
    D. set penalties for substandard performance

20. Assume that, because there has been an unexpected and temporary increase in the short-term work of your unit, you have had temporarily assigned to you several staff members from another agency.
    Of the following, in dealing with these employees, it would be LEAST advisable to
    A. assign them to long-term projects
    B. organize tasks so that they can begin work immediately
    C. set standards, making allowances to give them time to learn your ways
    D. direct them in the same way, in general, as you do your regular staff

21. It has been suggested that one way to increase employee productivity would be to require employees dealing with the public to have proficiency in a relevant foreign language.
    Of the following, the MAJOR reason for implementing such a proposal, from the viewpoint of effective public administration, would be to
    A. encourage the foreign-born to learn English
    B. exchange information more rapidly and accurately
    C. increase the public prestige of the agency
    D. stimulate ethnic pride among all groups

    21.____

22. Assume that the clerk who normally keeps your unit's records will be on vacation for four weeks.
    If other clerks are equally qualified to keep these records, your BEST choice to replace the clerk would be the person who
    A. has skills which are needed least for other duties during this period
    B. volunteers for this work
    C. is next in turn for a special assignment
    D. has handled this task before

    22.____

23. Assume that you have under your supervision several young clerical employees who have the bad habit of fooling around when they should be working.
    Of the following, the BEST disciplinary action to take would be to
    A. ignore it; these young people will outgrow it
    B. join in the fun briefly in order to bring it to a quicker end each time it occurs
    C. bring to their attention the fact that this behavior is not acceptable and if it continues shift the make-up of the group to keep these young persons apart
    D. warn them that this type of behavior is reason for dismissal and be quick to make an example of the first one who starts it again

    23.____

24. Seeking the advice of community leaders has human relations value for a public agency in planning or executing its programs CHIEFLY because it
    A. allows for the keeping of careful records concerning individual suggestions
    B. lets community leaders know that the agency has regard for their opinions
    C. permits the agency to state in writing which programs seem most appropriate
    D. unifies community leaders against the programs of competing private agencies

    24.____

25. Good community relations is often action-oriented.
    Which of the following activities of a public agency is LEAST likely to be considered as action-oriented by the people of a local community?
    A. Conducting a survey to gather information about the local community
    B. Extending the use of a facility to those previously excluded
    C. Providing a service that was formerly non-existent
    D. Removing something considered objectionable by the local community

    25.____

KEY (CORRECT ANSWERS)

1.	A	11.	D
2.	B	12.	B
3.	A	13.	C
4.	B	14.	A
5.	A	15.	B
6.	C	16.	C
7.	A	17.	D
8.	B	18.	D
9.	C	19.	D
10.	D	20.	A

21. B
22. A
23. C
24. B
25. A

TEST 2

DIRECTIONS: Each question or incomplete statement is followed by several suggested answers or completions. Select the one that BEST answers the question or completes the statement. *PRINT THE LETTER OF THE CORRECT ANSWER IN THE SPACE AT THE RIGHT.*

1. Methods of communication with employees are of three types: oral, written, and visual.
   A MAJOR advantage of the written word is that it
   A. insures that content will remain unchanged no matter how many persons may be involved in its transmission
   B. facilitates two-way communication in delicate or confidential situations
   C. strengthens chain-of-command procedures in transmission of information and instruction by requiring the use of prescribed channels
   D. encourages the active participation of employees in the solution of complicated problems

   1._____

2. The use of the conference technique in training often requires more preparatory work on the part of the trainer than does a good lecture PRIMARILY because
   A. a conference would cover material of a more technical nature
   B. the trainer will be required to supply more printed material to the participants
   C. a conference usually involves a greater number of trainees
   D. the trainer must be prepared for a wide variety of possible occurrences

   2._____

3. The one of the following which is NOT an advantage of the lecture over most other methods of training is that it can be given
   A. over the radio or on record   B. to large numbers of trainees
   C. without interruptions   D. with little preparation

   3._____

4. Of the following, the one which is LEAST appropriate as a purpose for using an employee attitude survey is to
   A. develop a supervisory training program
   B. learn the identity of dissatisfied employees
   C. re-evaluate employee relations policies
   D. re-orient publications designed for employees

   4._____

5. The competent trainer seeks to become knowledgeable both in the work of the agency and in the duties of the positions for which he is to conduct training. Of the following, the GREATEST practical value that result when the trainer gains such knowledge is that
   A. he will be more likely to instruct employees to perform their work in a manner consistent with actual practice
   B. all levels of staff will be favorably impressed by a display of interest in the agency and its work
   C. employees will become familiar with the trainer and will not consider him an outsider
   D. the trainer will gain an accurate picture of the capacity of each employee for training

   5._____

6. Assume that you, the supervisor of a small office, are involved in planning the reorganization of your bureau's work. Management has decided not to inform your staff of the reorganization until the plans are completed.
   If one of your subordinates tells you that he has heard a rumor about reorganization of the department, you should reply that
   A. the reorganization involves the bureau, not the department
   B. you haven't heard anything about departmental reorganization and that he should stop spreading rumors
   C. you will inform your staff at the appropriate time if any definite plans are made involving a reorganization
   D. you do not know what is being planned but will ask your superior for details

7. Of the following training methods, the one in which the trainee's role is usually LEAST active is the _____ method.
   A. case-study
   B. conference
   C. group discussion
   D. lecture

8. Differences in morale between two work groups can sometimes be attributed to differences in the supervision they receive.
   Of the following, the behavior MOST characteristic of a supervisor of a group with high morale is that he
   A. assigns the least difficult tasks to employees with the most seniority
   B. is concerned primarily with his ultimate responsibility, production
   C. delegates authority and responsibility to his staff
   D. is lenient with his workers when they violate rules

9. Informal performance evaluations of individual employees, prepared systematically and regularly over a period of several years, are considered to be useful to a supervisor PRIMARILY because
   A. he will be able to assign tasks based only on these records
   B. unlike formal records, since they are fitted to the characteristics of individual employees, they provide for quick comparisons
   C. he need not discuss them with employees, since they are informal
   D. whatever personnel action he recommends can be substantiated by cumulative records

10. When instructing first-line supervisors in the proper method of evaluating the performance of probationary employees, it is LEAST important for a higher-level supervisor to
    A. explain in detail the standards to be used
    B. inform them of the possibility of higher management review
    C. caution them concerning common errors of evaluation
    D. mention the purposes of probationary employee evaluation

11. Assume that your agency is considering abolishing its official performance rating system but that you, a supervisor of a fairly large office, would like to devise a system for your own use.
The FIRST step in setting up a system would be to
    A. decide what factors and personal characteristics are important and should be rated
    B. compare several rating methods to see which would be easiest to use
    C. have a private conference with each employee to discuss his performance
    D. set specific standards of employee performance, allowing your workers to make suggestions

11.____

12. The basic organizational structure of a municipal agency may have come about for several reasons.
Of the following, the MOST important influence on the nature of its structure is the agency's
    A. professional attitude
    B. public reputation
    C. overall goal
    D. staff morale

12.____

13. The term *formal organization* refers to that organization structure agreed upon by top management whereas the term *informal organization* refers to the more spontaneous and flexible organizational ties developed by subordinates.
The one of the following which BEST describes the usual *informal organization* is that it represents a(n)
    A. destructive system of relationships which should be eliminated
    B. concealed system of relationships whose goals are the same as management's
    C. actual system of relationships which should be recognized
    D. dysfunctional system of relationships which should be ignored

13.____

14. The reluctance of supervisors to delegate work to subordinates when they should is GENERALLY due to the supervisor's
    A. feelings of insecurity in work situations
    B. need to acquire additional experience
    C. inability to exercise control over his subordinates
    D. lack of technical knowledge

14.____

15. Assume that you have just been made the supervisor of a group of people you did not know before.
For you to talk casually with each of your new subordinates with the purpose of getting to know them personally would be
    A. *advisable*, chiefly because subordinates have more confidence in a supervisor who shows personal interest in them
    B. *inadvisable*, chiefly because subordinates resent having their supervisor ask about their outside interests
    C. *advisable*, chiefly because one of the supervisor's main concerns should be to help his subordinates with their personal problems
    D. *inadvisable*, chiefly because a supervisor should not allow his relations with his subordinates to be influenced by their personalities

15.____

16. It has been found that high-producing subdivisions of organizations usually have supervisors whose behavior is employee-centered, whereas low-producing units usually have supervisors whose behavior is work-centered.
    Therefore, it could be concluded from these findings that
    A. a high-producing unit may cause a supervisor to be authoritarian
    B. a low-producing unit may cause a supervisor to be work-centered
    C. close supervision usually increases production
    D. employee-centered leadership may reduce production

17. A recent study in managerial science showed that, as the amount of praise increased and amount of criticism decreased, the supervisor was more likely to be perceived by his subordinates as being
    A. concerned with their career advancement
    B. production oriented, through subtle intimidation
    C. seeking personal satisfaction, irrespective of production
    D. uncertain of the subordinates' reliability

18. The power to issue directives or instructions to employees is derived from employees as much as from management.
    It follows MOST logically from this statement that
    A. attitudes toward management can be changed
    B. emphasis on discipline is needed
    C. authority is dependent upon acceptance
    D. employees should be properly supervised for work to be done

19. "In the decision-making process, it is a rare problem that has only one possible solution. Such a solution should be suspected of being nothing but a plausible argument for a preconceived idea."
    The author of the foregoing quotation apparently does NOT believe that
    A. there is usually only one possible solution to a problem
    B. the risks involved in any solution should be weighed against expected gains
    C. each alternative should be evaluated to determine the effort needed
    D. actions should be based on the urgency of problems

20. The supervisor who relies on punitive discipline to enforce his authority is putting limits on the potential of his leadership. Fear of punishment may secure obedience, but it destroys initiative. Such a supervisor's autocratic methods have cut off upward communications.
    Of the following, the major DISADVANTAGE of such autocratic behavior is that
    A. difficulties in the supervision of his subordinates will arise if limits are placed on the supervisor's responsibility
    B. policies that affect the public will be changed too frequently
    C. the supervisor will apply punishment subjectively rather than objectively
    D. instructions will be obeyed to the letter, regardless of changing circumstances

21. The need for a supervisor to carefully coordinate and direct the work of his unit increases as the work becomes   21.____
    A. more routine
    B. more specialized
    C. less complex
    D. less technical

22. The MAIN goal of discipline as used by a supervisor should be to   22.____
    A. keep the employees' respect
    B. influence behavior, so that work will be completed properly
    C. encourage the employees to work faster
    D. set an example for others

23. One of your subordinates has exhibited discourtesy and non-cooperation on several occasions.   23.____
    Of the following, the MOST appropriate attitude for you to adopt in dealing with this problem is that
    A. disciplinary measures for such an individual generally creates additional problems
    B. failure to correct such behavior may lead to worse offenses
    C. it is a mistake to make an issue out of minor infractions
    D. the harsher the medicine, the faster the cure

24. Assume that an employee has complained to you, his supervisor, that he cannot concentrate on his work because two of his co-workers make too much noise. You pay particular attention to these employees for several days and do not find them making excessive noise.   24.____
    The NEXT step you should take in handling this grievance is to
    A. have a talk with all three employees, urging them to cooperate and be considerate of one another
    B. arrange for the complainant to change his work location to a place away from the two co-workers
    C. talk to the complainant to find out if the complaint he made to you is the real cause of his dissatisfaction
    D. tell the complainant that you have found his grievance to be unfounded

25. In planning the application of an existing agency program to a local community, it is generally necessary to discover relevant problems and possibilities for service.   25.____
    Of the following, the BEST way to learn about such problems and possibilities for service would usually be to
    A. begin the program on a full-scale basis and await reactions
    B. seek opinions and advice from community residents and leaders
    C. hold staff meetings with agency employees who have worked in similar communities
    D. study official federal reports about already completed programs of the same kind

KEY (CORRECT ANSWERS)

1. A
2. D
3. D
4. B
5. A

6. C
7. D
8. C
9. D
10. B

11. A
12. C
13. C
14. A
15. A

16. B
17. A
18. C
19. A
20. D

21. B
22. B
23. B
24. C
25. B

TEST 3

DIRECTIONS: Each question or incomplete statement is followed by several suggested answers or completions. Select the one that BEST answers the question or completes the statement. *PRINT THE LETTER OF THE CORRECT ANSWER IN THE SPACE AT THE RIGHT.*

1. Which of the following characteristics would be LEAST detrimental to a supervisor in his efforts to set up and maintain good relations with other supervisors with whom he must deal in the course of his duties?
   A. Not getting involved in consultation on any supervisory problems they might have
   B. Indicating that they should improve their supervising methods and offering suggestions on how to do so
   C. Emphasizing his own role as a member of management
   D. Sharing information which has proved useful in his unit

   1.____

2. Both trainers and supervisors might agree that there is usually a best way to do a particular job. Yet a supervisor or instructor sometimes does not teach a new employee the best way, the most efficient way, to do a complex job.
   Sometimes, in such cases, the supervisor temporarily changes the sequence of operations, increases the number of steps needed to do a job, or makes other changes in the method, which then deviates from the one considered most efficient.
   When is such a difference in approach MOST justified when teaching a new employee a complex job?
   A. When the changes in approach correspond to the learning ability of the new employee
   B. When the new employee's performance on the job is closely supervised to compensate for a change in approach
   C. Where the steps in performing the task have not been defined in a manual of procedures
   D. When the instructor has ideas of improving upon the methods for doing the job

   2.____

3. Considerable thought in the field of management is directed toward the advantages and disadvantages of authoritarian methods of influencing behavior, and, in the so-called authoritarian model, a nucleus of rather consistent ideas prevail.
   Which of the following is LEAST characteristic of an administrative system based on the authoritarian model?
   A. A conviction of a need for order and efficiency in a world consisting mainly of people who lack direction and incentive
   B. Rules and contracts are the basis for action, and decisions are made on an impersonal basis
   C. The right to give orders and instructions is inherent in the hierarchical arrangement of an organizational structure
   D. Realization that subordinates' needs for affiliation and recognition can contribute to management's objectives

   3.____

4. Of the following, the FIRST step in planning an operation is to
   A. obtain relevant information
   B. identify the goal to be achieved
   C. consider possible alternatives
   D. make necessary assignments

5. A supervisor who is extremely busy performing routine tasks is MOST likely making incorrect use of what basis principle of supervision?
   A. Homogeneous Assignment
   B. Span of Control
   C. Work Distribution
   D. Delegation of Authority

6. Controls help supervisors to obtain information from which they can determine whether their staffs are achieving planned goals.
   Which one of the following would be LEAST useful as a control device?
   A. Employee diaries
   B. Organization charts
   C. Periodic inspections
   D. Progress charts

7. A certain employee has difficulty in effectively performing a particular portion of his routine assignments, but his overall productivity is average.
   As a direct supervisor of this individual, your BEST course of action would be to
   A. attempt to develop the investigator's capacity to execute the problematical facets of his assignments
   B. diversify the investigator's work assignments in order to build up his confidence
   C. reassign the investigator to less difficult tasks
   D. request in a private conversation that the investigator improve his work output

8. A supervisor who uses persuasion as a means of supervising a unit would GENERALLY also use which of the following practices to supervise his unit?
   A. Supervises and control the staff with an authoritative attitude to indicate that he is a *take-charge* individual
   B. Make significant changes in the organizational operations so as to improve job efficiency
   C. Remove major communication barriers between himself, subordinates, and management
   D. Supervise everyday operations while being mindful of the problems of his subordinates

9. Whenever a supervisor in charge of a unit delegates a routine task to a capable subordinate, he tells him exactly how to do it.
   This practice is GENERALLY
   A. *desirable*, chiefly because good supervisors should be aware of the traits of their subordinates and delegate responsibilities to them accordingly
   B. *undesirable*, chiefly because only non-routine tasks should be delegated
   C. *desirable*, chiefly because a supervisor should frequently test the willingness of his subordinates to perform ordinary tasks
   D. *undesirable*, chiefly because a capable subordinate should usually be allowed to exercise his own discretion in doing a routine job

10. The one of the following activities through which a supervisor BEST demonstrates leadership ability is by
    A. arranging periodic staff meetings in order to keep his subordinates informed about professional developments in the field of investigation
    B. frequently issuing definite orders and directives which will lessen the need for subordinates to make decisions in handling any investigations assigned to them
    C. devoting the major part of his time to supervising subordinates so as to stimulate continuous improvement
    D. setting aside time for self-development and research so as to improve the investigative techniques and procedures of his unit

11. The following three statements relate to supervision of employees:
    I. The assignment of difficult tasks that offer a challenge is more conducive to good morale than the assignment of easy tasks.
    II. The same general principles of supervision that apply to men are equally applicable to women.
    III. The best restraining program should cover all phases of an employee's work in a general manner.
    Which of the following choices lists ALL of the above statements that are generally CORRECT?
    A. II, III   B. I   C. I, II   D. I, II, III

12. Which of the following examples BEST illustrates the application of the *exception principle* as a supervisory technique? A(n)
    A. complex job is divided among several employees who work simultaneously to complete the whole job in a shorter time
    B. employee is required to complete any task delegated to him to such an extent that nothing is left for the superior who delegated the task except to approve it
    C. superior delegates responsibility to a subordinate but retains authority to make the final decisions
    D. superior delegates all work possible to his subordinates and retains that which requires his personal attention or performance

13. Assume that you are a supervisor. Your immediate superior frequently gives orders to your subordinates without your knowledge.
    Of the following, the MOST direct and effective way for you to handle this problem is to
    A. tell your subordinates to take orders only from you
    B. submit a report to higher authority in which you cite specific instances
    C. discuss it with your immediate superior
    D. find out to what extent you authority and prestige as a supervisor have been affected

14. In an agency which has as its primary purpose the protection of the public against fraudulent business practices, which of the following would GENERALLY be considered an auxiliary or staff rather than a line function?

A. Interviewing victims of frauds and advising them about their legal remedies
B. Daily activities directed toward prevention of fraudulent business practices
C. Keeping records and statistics about business violations reported and corrected
D. Follow-up inspections by investigators after corrective action has been taken

15. A supervisor can MOST effectively reduce the spread of false rumors through the *grapevine* by
    A. identifying and disciplining any subordinate responsible for initiating such rumors
    B. keeping his subordinates informed as much as possible about matters affecting them
    C. denying false rumors which might tend to lower staff morale and productivity
    D. making sure confidential matters are kept secure from access by unauthorized employees

15.____

16. A supervisor has tried to learn about the background, education, and family relationships of his subordinates through observation, personal contact, and inspection of their personnel records.
    These supervisory actions are GENERALLY
    A. *inadvisable*, chiefly because they may lead to charges of favoritism
    B. *advisable*, chiefly because they may make him more popular with his subordinates
    C. *inadvisable*, chiefly because his efforts may be regarded as an invasion of privacy
    D. *advisable*, chiefly because the information may enable him to develop better understanding of each of his subordinates

16.____

17. In an emergency situation, when action must be taken immediately, it is BEST for the supervisor to give orders in the form of
    A. direct commands, which are brief and precise
    B. requests, so that his subordinate will not become alarmed
    C. suggestions, which offer alternative courses of action
    D. implied directive, so that his subordinates may use their judgment in carrying them out

17.____

18. When demonstrating a new and complex procedure to a group of subordinates, it is ESSENTIAL that a supervisor
    A. go slowly and repeat the steps involved at least once
    B. show the employees common errors and the consequences of such errors
    C. go through the process at the usual speed so that the employees can see the rate at which they should work
    D. distribute summaries of the procedure during the demonstration and instruct his subordinates to refer to them afterwards

18.____

19. The PRIMARY value of office reports and procedures is to
    A. assist top management in controlling key agency functions
    B. measure job performance
    C. save time and labor
    D. control the activities and use of time of all staff members

20. Of the following, which is considered to be the GREATEST advantage of the oral report? It
    A. allows for accurate transmission of information from one individual to another
    B. presents an opportunity to discuss or clarify any immediate questions raised by the receiver of the report
    C. requires less office work to maintain records on actions taken when an oral report is involved
    D. takes only a short amount of time to plan and prepare material for an oral report

21. A supervisor who is to make a report about a job he has done can make an oral report of a written report.
    Of the following, which is the BEST time to make an oral report? When
    A. the work covers an emergency situation
    B. a record is needed for the files
    C. the report is channeled to other departments
    D. the report covers additional work he will do

22. Suppose that a new employee has been assigned to you. It is your responsibility to see to it that he understands how to fill out properly the forms he is required to use.
    What would be the BEST way to do this?
    A. Explain the use of each form to the new technician and show him how to fill them out
    B. Give the new employee a copy of each form he must use so that he can learn by studying them
    C. Ask an experienced worker to explain clearly to him how the forms should be filled out
    D. Tell the new employee that filling out forms is simple and he should follow the instructions on each form

23. As a supervisor, you want to have your staff take part in improving work methods.
    Of the following, the BEST way to do this is to
    A. make critical appraisals of their work frequently
    B. encourage them to make suggestions
    C. make no change without their approval
    D. hold regular staff meetings

24. A good relationship with other supervisors is important to a senior supervisor. Close cooperation among supervisory personnel is MOST likely to result in
    A. increasing the probability for support of supervisory actions and decisions
    B. stimulating supervisors to achieve higher status in the organization
    C. helping to control the flow of work within a unit
    D. a clearer definition of the responsibilities of individual supervisors

25. Which of the following is MOST likely to gain a supervisor the respect and cooperation of his staff?
    A. Assigning the most difficult jobs to the experienced staff members
    B. Giving each staff member the same number of assignments
    C. Assigning jobs according to each staff member's ability
    D. Giving each staff member the same types of assignments

KEY (CORRECT ANSWERS)

1.	D	11.	C
2.	A	12.	D
3.	D	13.	C
4.	B	14.	C
5.	D	15.	B
6.	B	16.	D
7.	A	17.	A
8.	D	18.	A
9.	D	19.	A
10.	C	20.	B

21.	A
22.	A
23.	B
24.	A
25.	C

SUPERVISION STUDY GUIDE

Social science has developed information about groups and leadership in general and supervisor-employee relationships in particular. Since organizational effectiveness is closely linked to the ability of supervisors to direct the activities of employees, these findings are important to executives everywhere.

IS A SUPERVISOR A LEADER?

First-line supervisors are found in all large business and government organizations. They are the men at the base of an organizational hierarchy. Decisions made by the head of the organization reach them through a network of intermediate positions. They are frequently referred to as part of the management team, but their duties seldom seem to support this description.

A supervisor of clerks, tax collectors, meat inspectors, or securities analysts is not charged with budget preparation. He cannot hire or fire the employees in his own unit on his say-so. He does not administer programs which require great planning, coordinating, or decision making.

Then what is he? He is the man who is directly in charge of a group of employees doing productive work for a business or government agency. If the work requires the use of machines, the men he supervises operate them. If the work requires the writing of reports, the men he supervises write them. He is expected to maintain a productive flow of work without creating problems which higher levels of management must solve. But is he a leader?

To carry out a specific part of an agency's mission, management creates a unit, staffs it with a group of employees and designates a supervisor to take charge of them. Management directs what this unit shall do, from time to time changes directions, and often indicates what the group should not do. Management presumably creates status for the supervisor by giving him more pay, a title, and special privileges.

Management asks a supervisor to get his workers to attain organizational goals, including the desired quantity and quality of production. Supposedly, he has authority to enable him to achieve this objective. Management at least assumes that by establishing the status of the supervisor's position, it has created sufficient authority to enable him to achieve these goals— not his goals, nor necessarily the group's, but management's goals.

In addition, supervision includes writing reports, keeping records of membership in a higher-level administrative group, industrial engineering, safety engineering, editorial duties, housekeeping duties, etc. The supervisor as a member of an organizational network, must be responsible to the changing demands of the management above him. At the same time, he must be responsive to the demands of the work group of which he is a member. He is placed in the difficult position of communicating and implementing new decisions, changed programs and revised production quotas for his work group, although he may have had little part in developing them.

It follows, then, that supervision has a special characteristic: achievement of goals, previously set by management, through the efforts of others. It is in this feature of the supervisor's job that we find the role of a leader in the sense of the following definition: *A leader is that person who <u>most</u> effectively influences group activities toward goal setting and goal achievements.*

This definition is broad. It covers both leaders in groups that come together voluntarily and in those brought together through a work assignment in a factory, store, or government agency. In the natural group, the authority necessary to attain goals is determined by the group membership and is granted by them. In the working group, it is apparent that the establishment of a supervisory position creates a predisposition on the part of employees to accept the authority of the occupant of that position. We cannot, however, assume that mere occupation confers authority sufficient to assure the accomplishment of an organization's goals.

Supervision is different, then, from leadership. The supervisor is expected to fulfill the role of leader but without obtaining a grant of authority from the group he supervises. The supervisor is expected to influence the group in the achieving of goals but is often handicapped by having little influence on the organizational process by which goals are set. The supervisor, because he works in an organizational setting, has the burdens of additional organizational duties and restrictions and requirements arising out of the fact that his position is subordinate to a hierarchy of higher-level supervisors. These differences between leadership and supervision are reflected in our definition: *Supervision is basically a leadership role, in a formal organization, which has as its objective the effective influencing of other employees.*

Even though these differences between supervision and leadership exist, a significant finding of experimenters in this field is that supervisors <u>must</u> be leaders to be successful.

The problem is: How can a supervisor exercise leadership in an organizational setting? We might say that the supervisor is expected to be a natural leader in a situation which does not come about naturally. His situation becomes really difficult in an organization which is more eager to make its supervisors into followers rather than leaders.

LEADERSHIP: NATURAL AND ORGANIZATIONAL

Leadership, in its usual sense of *natural* leadership, and supervision are not the same. In some cases, leadership embraces broader powers and functions than supervision; in other cases, supervision embraces more than leadership. This is true both because of the organization and technical aspects of the supervisor's job and because of the relatively freer setting and inherent authority of the natural leader.

The natural leader usually has much more authority and influence than the supervisor. Group members not only follow his command but prefer it that way. The employee, however, can appeal the supervisor's commands to his union or to the supervisor's superior or to the personnel office. These intercessors represent restrictions on the supervisor's power to lead.

The natural leader can gain greater membership involvement in the group's objectives, and he can change the objectives of the group. The supervisor can attempt to gain employee support only for management's objectives; he cannot set other objectives. In these instances leadership is broader than supervision.

The natural leader must depend upon whatever skills are available when seeking to attain objectives. The supervisor is trained in the administrative skills necessary to achieve management's goals. If he does not possess the requisite skills, however, he can call upon management's technicians.

A natural leader can maintain his leadership, in certain groups, merely by satisfying members' need for group affiliation. The supervisor must maintain his leadership by directing and organizing his group to achieve specific organizational goals set for him and his group by management. He must have a technical competence and a kind of coordinating ability which is not needed by many natural leaders.

A natural leader is responsible only to his group which grants him authority. The supervisor is responsible to management, which employs him, and also to the work group of which he is a member. The supervisor has the exceedingly difficult job of reconciling the demands of two groups frequently in conflict. He is often placed in the untenable position of trying to play two antagonistic roles. In the above instance, supervision is broader than leadership.

ORGANIZATIONAL INFLUENCES ON LEADERSHIP

The supervisor is both a product and a prisoner of the organization wherein we find him. The organization which creates the supervisor's position also obstructs, restricts, and channelizes the exercise of his duties. These influences extend beyond prescribed functional relationships to specific supervisory behavior. For example, even in a face-to-face situation involving one of his subordinates, the supervisor's actions are controlled to a great extent by his organization. His behavior must conform to the organization policy on human relations, rules which dictate personnel procedures, specific prohibitions governing conduct, the attitudes of his own superior, etc. He is not a free agent operating within the limits of his work group. His freedom of action is much more circumscribed than is generally admitted. The organizational influences which limit his leadership actions can be classified as structure, prescriptions, and proscriptions.

The organizational structure places each supervisor's position in context with other designated positions. It determines the relationships between his position and specific positions which impinge on his. The structure of the organization designates a certain position to which he looks for orders and information about his work. It gives a particular status to his position within a pattern of statuses from which he perceives that (1) certain positions are on a par, organizationally, with his, (2) other positions are subordinate, and (3) still others are superior.

The organizational structure determines those positions to which he should look for advice and assistance, and those positions to which he should give advice and assistance.

For instance, the organizational structure has predetermined that the supervisor of a clerical processing unit shall report to a supervisory position in a higher echelon. He shall have certain relationships with the supervisors of the work units which transmit work to and receive work from his unit. He shall discuss changes and clarification of procedures with certain staff units, such as organization and methods, cost accounting, and personnel. He shall consult supervisors of units which provide or receive special work assignments.

The organizational structure, however, establishes patterns other than those of the relationships of positions. These are the patterns of responsibility, authority, and expectations.

The supervisor is responsible for certain activities or results; he is presumably invested with the authority to achieve these. His set of authority and responsibility is interwoven with other sets to the end that all goals and functions of the organization are parceled out in small, manageable lots. This, of course, establishes a series of expectations: a single supervisor can perform his particular set of duties only upon the assumption that preceding or contiguous sets of duties have been, or are being carried out. At the same time, he is aware of the expectations of others that he will fulfill his functional role.

The structure of an organization establishes relationships between specified positions and specific expectations for these positions. The fact that these relationships and expectations are established is one thing; whether or not they are met is another.

PRESCRIPTIONS AND PROSCRIPTIONS

But let us return to the organizational influences which act to restrict the supervisor's exercise of leadership. These are the prescriptions and proscriptions generally in effect in all organizations, and those peculiar to a single organization. In brief these are the *thou shalt's* and the *thou shalt not's*.

Organizations not only prescribe certain duties for individual supervisory positions, they also prescribe specific methods and means of carrying out these duties and maintaining management-employee relations. These include rules, regulations, policy, and tradition. It does no good for the supervisor to say, *This seems to be the best way to handle such-and-such,* if the organization has established a routine for dealing with problems. For good or bad, there are rules that state that firings shall be executed in such a manner, accompanied by a certain notification; that training shall be conducted, and in this manner. Proscriptions are merely negative prescriptions; you may not discriminate against any employee because of politics or race; you shall not suspend any employee without following certain procedures and obtaining certain approvals.

Most of these prohibitions and rules apply to the area of interpersonal relations, precisely the area which is now arousing most interest on the part of administrators and managers. We have become concerned about the contrast between formally prescribed relationships and interpersonal relationships, and this brings us to the often discussed informal organization.

FORMAL AND INFORMAL ORGANIZATIONS

As we well know, the functions and activities of any organization are broken down into individual units of work called positions. Administrators must establish a pattern which will link these positions to each other and relate them to a system of authority and responsibility. Man-to-man are spelled out as plainly as possible for all to understand. Managers, then, build an official structure which we call the formal organization.

In these same organizations, employees react individually and in groups to institutionally determined roles. John, a worker, rides in the same carpool as Joe, a foreman. An unplanned communication develops. Harry, a machinist knows more about high-speed machining than his foreman or anyone else in his shop. An unofficial tool boss comes into being. Mary, who fought with Jane, is promoted over her. Jane now gives Mary's directions. A planned relationship fails to develop. The employees have built a structure which we call the informal organization.

Formal organization is a system of management-prescribed relations between positions in an organization.

Informal organization is a network of unofficial relations between people in an organization.

These definitions might lead us to the absurd conclusion that positions carry out formal activities and that employe4es spend their time in unofficial activities. We must recognize that organizational activities are in all cases carried out by people. The formal structure provides a needed framework within which interpersonal relations occur. What we call informal organization is the complex of normal, natural relations among employees. These personal relationships may be negative or positive. That is, they may impede or aid the achievement of organizational goals. For example, friendship between two supervisors greatly increases the probability of good cooperation and coordination between their sections. On the other hand, *buck passing* nullifies the formal structure by failure to meet a prescribed and expected responsibility.

It is improbable that an ideal organization exists where all activities are carried out in strict conformity to a formally prescribed pattern of functional roles. Informal organization arises because of the incompleteness and ambiguities in the network of formally prescribed relationships, or in response to the needs or inadequacies of supervisors or managers who hold prescribed functional roles in an organization. Many of these relationships are not prescribed by the organizational pattern; many cannot be prescribed; many should not be prescribed.

Management faces the problem of keeping the informal organization in harmony with the mission of the agency. One way to do this is to make sure that all employees have a clear understanding of and are sympathetic with that mission. The issuance of organizational charts, procedural manuals, and functional descriptions of the work to be done by divisions and sections helps communicate management's plans and goals. Issuances alone, of course, cannot do the whole job. They should be accompanied by oral discussion and explanation. Management must ensure that there is mutual understanding and acceptance of charts and procedures. More important is that management acquaint itself with the attitudes, activities, and peculiar brands of logic which govern the informal organization. Only through this type of knowledge can they and supervisors keep informal goals consistent with the agency mission.

SUPERVISION STATUS AND FUNCTIONAL ROLE

A well-established supervisor is respected by the employees who work with him. They defer to his wishes. It is clear that a superior-subordinate relationship has been established. That is, status of the supervisor has been established in relation to other employees of the same work group. This same supervisor gains the respect of employees when he behaves in as certain manner. He will be expected, generally, to follow the customs of the group in such matters as dress, recreation, and manner of speaking. The group has a set of expectations as to his behavior. His position is a functional role which carries with it a collection of rights and obligations.

The position of supervisor usually has a status distinct from the individual who occupies it: it is much like a position description which exists whether or not there is an incumbent. The status of a supervisory position is valued higher than that of an employee position both because of the functional role of leadership which is assigned to it and because of the status symbols of titles, rights, and privileges which go with it.

Social ranking, or status, is not simple because it involves both the position and the man. An individual may be ranked higher than others because of his education, social background, perceived leadership ability, or conformity to group customs and ideals. If such a man is ranked higher by the members of a work group than their supervisor, the supervisor's effectiveness may be seriously undermined.

If the organization does not build and reinforce a supervisor's status, his position can be undermined in a different way. This will happen when managers go around rather than through the supervisor or designate him as a straw boss, acting boss, or otherwise not a real boss.

Let us clarify this last point. A role, and corresponding status, establishes a set of expectations. Employees expect their supervisor to do certain things and to act in certain ways. They are prepared to respond to that expected behavior. When the supervisor's behavior does not conform to their expectations, they are surprised, confused, and ill-at-ease. It becomes necessary for them to resolve their confusion, if they can. They might do this by turning to one of their own members for leadership. If the confusion continues, or their attempted solutions are not satisfactory, they will probably become a poorly motivated, non-cohesive group which cannot function very well.

COMMUNICATION AND THE SUPERVISOR

In a recent survey, railroad workers reported that they rarely look to their supervisor for information about the company. This is startling, at least to us, because we ordinarily think of the supervisor as the link between management and worker. We expect the supervisor to be the prime source of information about the company. Actually, the railroad workers listed the supervisor next to last in the o5rder of their sources of information. Most surprising of all, the supervisors, themselves, stated that rumor and unofficial contacts were their principal sources of information. Here we see one of the reasons why supervisors may not be as effective as management desires.

The supervisor is not only being bypassed by his work group, he is being ignored, and his position weakened, by the very organization which is holding him responsible for the activities of his workers. If he is management's representative to the employee, then management has an obligation to keep him informed of its activities. This is necessary if he is to carry out his functions efficiently and maintain his leadership in the work group. The supervisor is expected to be a source of information; when he is not, his status is not clear, and employees are dissatisfied because he has not lived up to expectations.

By providing information to the supervisor to pass along to employees, we can strengthen his position as leader of the group, and increase satisfaction and cohesion within the group. Because he has more information than the other members, receives information sooner, and passes it along at the proper times, members turn to him as a source and also provide him with information in the hope of receiving some in return. From this, we can see an increase in group cohesiveness because:

- Employees are bound closer to their supervisor because he is *in the know*.
- There is less need to go outside the group for answers
- Employees will more quickly turn to the supervisor for enlightenment

The fact that he has the answers will also enhance the supervisor's standing in the eyes of his men. This increased status will serve to bolster his authority and control of the group and will probably result in improved morale and productivity.

The foregoing, of course, does not mean that all management information should be given out. There are obviously certain policy determinations and discussions which need not or cannot be transmitted to all supervisors. However, the supervisor must be kept as fully informed as possible so that he can answer questions when asked and can allay needless fears and anxieties. Further, the supervisor has the responsibility of encouraging employee questions and submissions of information. He must be able to present information to employees so that it is clearly understood and accepted. His attitude and manner should make it clear that he believes in what he is saying, that the information is necessary or desirable to the group, and that he is prepared to act on the basis of the information.

SUPERVISION AND JOB PERFORMANCE

The productivity of work groups is a product; employees' efforts are multiplied by the supervision they receive. Many investigators have analyzed this relationship and have discovered elements of supervision which differentiate high and low production groups. These researchers have identified certain types of supervisory practices which they classify as *employee-centered* and other types which they classify as *production centered*.

The difference between these two kinds of supervision lies not in specific practices but in the approach or orientation to supervision. The employee-centered supervisor directs most of his efforts toward increasing employee motivation. He is concerned more with realizing the potential energy of persons than with administrative and technological methods of increasing efficiency and productivity. He is the man who finds ways of causing employees to want to work harder with the same tools. These supervisors emphasize the personal relations between their employees and themselves.

Now, obviously, these pictures are overdrawn. No one supervisor has all the virtues of the ideal type of employee-centered supervisor. And, fortunately, no one supervisor has all the bad traits found in many production-centered supervisors. We should remember that the various practices that researchers have fond which distinguish these two kinds of supervision represent the many practices and methods of supervisors of all gradations between these extremes. We should be careful, too, of the implications of the labels attached to the two types. For instance, being production-centered is not necessarily bad, since the principal responsibility of any supervisor is maintaining the production level that is expected of his work group. Being employee-centered may not necessarily be good, if the only result is a happy, chuckling crew of loafers. To return to the researchers' findings, employee-centered supervisors:

- Recommend promotions, transfers, pay increases
- Inform men about what is happening in the company
- Keep men posted on how well they are doing
- Hear complaints and grievances sympathetically
- Speak up for subordinates

Production-centered supervisors, on the other hand, don't do those things. They check on employees more frequently, give more detailed and frequent instructions, don't give reasons for changes, and are more punitive when mistakes are made. Employee-centered supervisors were reported to contribute to high morale and high production, whereas production-centered supervision was associated with lower morale and less production.

More recent findings, however, show that the relationship between supervision and productivity is not this simple. Investigators now report that high production is more frequently associated with supervisory practices which combine employee-centered behavior with concern for production. (This concern is not the same, however, as anxiety about production, which is the hallmark of our production-centered supervisor.) Let us examine these apparently contradictory findings and the premises from which they are derived.

SUPERVISION AND MORALE

Why do supervisory activities cause high or low production? As the name implies, the activities of the employee-centered supervisor tend to relate him more closely and satisfactorily to his workers. The production-centered supervisor's practices tend to separate him from his group and to foster antagonism. An analysis of this difference may answer our question.

Earlier, we pointed out that the supervisor is a type of leader and that leadership is intimately related to the group in which it occurs We discover, now, that an employee-centered supervisor's primary activities are concerned with both his leadership and his group membership. Such a supervisor is a member of a group and occupies a leadership role in that group.

These facts are sometimes obscured when we speak of the supervisor as management's representative, or as the organizational link between management and the employee, or as the end of the chain of command. If we really want to understand what it is we expect of the supervisor, we must remember that he is the designated leader of a group of employees to whom he is bound by interaction and interdependence.

Most of his actions are aimed, consciously or unconsciously, at strengthening membership ties in the group. This includes both making members more conscious that he is a member of their group) and causing members to identify themselves more closely with the group. These ends are accomplished by:

- making the group more attractive to the worker: they find satisfaction of their needs for recognition, friendship, enjoyable work, etc.;
- maintaining open communication: employees can express their views and obtain information about the organization
- giving assistance: members can seek advice on personal problems as well as their work; and
- acting as a buffer between the group and management: he speaks up for his men and explains the reasons for management's decisions.

Such actions both strengthen group cohesiveness and solidarity and affirm the supervisor's leadership position in the group.

DEFINING MORALE

This brings us back to a point mentioned earlier. We had said that employee-centered supervisors contribute to high morale as well as to high production. But how can we explain units which have low morale and high productivity, or vice versa? Usually production and morale are considered separately, partly because they are measured against different criteria and partly because, in some instances, they seem to be independent of each other.

Some of this difficulty may stem from confusion over definitions of morale. Morale has been defined as, or measured by, absences from work, satisfaction with job or company, dissension among members of work groups, productivity, apathy or lack of interest, readiness to help others, and a general aura of happiness as rated by observers. Some of these criteria of morale are not subject to the influence of the supervisor, and some of them are not clearly related to productivity. Definitions like these invite findings of low morale coupled with high production.

Both productivity and morale can be influenced by environmental factors not under the control of group members or supervisors. Such things as plant layout, organizational structure and goals, lighting, ventilation, communications, and management planning may have an adverse or desirable effect.

We might resolve the dilemma by defining morale on the basis of our understanding of the supervisor as leader of a group; morale is the degree of satisfaction of group members with their leadership. In this light, the supervisor's employee-centered activities bear a clear relation to morale. His efforts to increase employee identification with the group and to strengthen his leadership lead to greater satisfaction with that leadership. By increasing group cohesiveness and by demonstrating that his influence and power can aid the group, he is able to enhance his leadership status and afford satisfaction to the group.

SUPERVISION, PRODUCTION, AND MORALE

There are factors within the organization itself which determine whether increased production is possible:

- Are production goals expressed in terms understandable to employees and are they realistic?
- Do supervisors responsible for production respect the agency mission and production goals?
- If employees do not know how to do the job well, does management provide a trainer—often the supervisor—who can teach efficient work methods?

There are other factors within the work group which determine whether increased production will be attained:

- Is leadership present which can bring about the desired level of production?
- Are production goals accepted by employees as reasonable and attainable?
- If group effort is involved, are members able to coordinate their efforts?

Research findings confirm the view that an employee-centered supervisor can achieve higher morale than a production-centered supervisor. Managers may well ask what is the relationship between this and production.

Supervision is production-oriented to the extent that it focuses attention on achieving organizational goals, and plans and devises methods for attaining them; it is employee-centered to the extent that it focuses attention on employee attitudes toward those goals, and plans and works toward maintenance of employee satisfaction.

High productivity and low morale result when a supervisor plans and organizes work efficiently but cannot achieve high membership satisfaction. Low production and high morale result when a supervisor, though keeping members satisfied with his leadership, either has not gained acceptance of organizational goals or does not have the technical competence to achieve them.

The relationship between supervision, morale, and productivity is an interdependent one, with the supervisor playing an integral role due to his ability to influence productivity and morale independently of each other.

A supervisor who can plan his work well has good technical knowledge, and who can install better production methods can raise production without necessarily increasing group satisfaction. On the other hand, a supervisor who can motivate his employees and keep them satisfied with his leadership can gain high production in spite of technical difficulties and environmental obstacles.

CLIMATE AND SUPERVISION

Climate, the intangible environment of an organization made up of attitudes, beliefs, and traditions, plays a large part in morale, productivity, and supervision. Usually when we speak of climate and its relationship to morale and productivity, we talk about the merits of *democratic* versus *authoritarian* climate. Employees seem to produce more and have higher morale in a democratic climate, whereas in an authoritarian climate, the reverse seems to be true or so the researchers tell us. We would do well to determine what these terms mean to supervision.

Perhaps most of our difficulty in understanding and applying these concepts comes from our emotional reactions to the words themselves. For example, authoritarian climate is usually painted as the very blackest kind of dictatorship. This is not surprising, because we are usually expected to believe that it is invariably bad. Conversely, democratic climate is drawn to make the driven snow look impure by comparison.

Now these descriptions are most probably true when we talk about our political processes, or town meetings, or freedom of speech. However, the same labels have been used by social scientists in other contexts and have also been applied to government and business organizations, without it, it seems, any recognition that the meanings and their social values may have changed somewhat

For example, these labels were used in experiments conducted in an informal classroom setting using 11-year-old boys as subjects. The descriptive labels applied to the climate of the setting as well as the type of leadership practiced. When these labels were transferred to a management setting, it seems that many presumed that they principally meant the king of leadership rather than climate. We can see that there is a great difference between the experimental and management settings and that leadership practices for one might be inappropriate for the other.

It is doubtful that formal work organizations can be anything but authoritarian, in that goals are set by management and a hierarchy exists through which decisions and orders from the top are transmitted downward. Organizations are authoritarian by structure and need; direction and control are placed in the hands of a few in order to gain fast and efficient decision making. Now this does not mean to describe a dictatorship. It is merely the recognition of the fact that direction of organizational affairs comes from above. It should be noted that leadership in some natural groups is, in this sense, authoritarian.

Granting that formal organizations have this kind of authoritarian leadership, can there be a democratic climate? Certainly there can be, but we would want to define and delimit this term. A more realistic meaning of democratic climate in organizations is the use of permissive and participatory methods in management-employee relations. That is, a mutual exchange of information and explanation with the granting of individual freedom within certain restricted and defined limits. However, it is not our purpose to debate the merits of authoritarianism versus democracy. We recognize that within the small work group there is a need for freedom from constraint and an increase in participation in order to achieve organizational goals within the framework of the organizational movement.

Another aspect of climate is best expressed by this familiar, and true, saying: actions speak louder than words. Of particular concern to us is this effect of management climate on the behavior of supervisors, particularly in employee-centered activities.

There have been reports of disappointment with efforts to make supervisors ore employee-centered. Managers state that, since research has shown ways of improving human relations, supervisors should begin to practice these methods. Usually a training course in human relations is established; and supervisors are given this training. Managers then sit back and wait for the expected improvements, only to find that there are none.

If we wish to produce changes in the supervisor's behavior, the climate must be made appropriate and rewarding to the changed behavior. This means that top-level attitudes and behavior cannot deny or contradict the change we are attempting to effect. Basic changes in organizational behavior cannot be made with any permanence, unless we provide an environment that is receptive to the changes and rewards those persons who do change.

IMPROVING SUPERVISION

Anyone who has read this far might expect to find *A Dozen Rules for Dealing With Employees* or *29 Steps to Supervisory Success*. We will not provide such a list.

Simple rules suffer from their simplicity. They ignore the complexities of human behavior. Reliance upon rules may cause supervisors to concentrate on superficial aspects of their relations with employees. It may preclude genuine understanding.

The supervisor who relies on a list of rules tends to think of people in mechanistic terms. In a certain situation, he uses *Rule No. 3*. Employees are not treated as thinking and feeling persons, but rather as figures in a formula: Rule 3 applied to employee X = Production.

Employees usually recognize mechanical manipulation and become dissatisfied and resentful. They lose faith in, and respect for, their supervisor, and this may be reflected in lower morale and productivity.

We do not mean that supervisors must become social science experts if they wish to improve. Reports of current research indicate that there are two major parts of their job which can be strengthened through self-improvement: (1) Work planning, including technical skills, and (2) motivation of employees.

The most effective supervisors combine excellence in the administrative and technical aspects of their work with friendly and considerate personal relations with their employees.

CRITICAL PERSONAL RELATIONS

Later in this chapter we shall talk about administrative aspects of supervision, but first let us comment on *friendly and considerate personal relations*. We have discussed this subject throughout the preceding chapters, but we want to review some of the critical supervisory influences on personal relations.

Closeness of Supervision: The closeness of supervision has an important effect on productivity and morale. Mann and Dent found that supervisors of low-producing units supervise very closely, while high-producing supervisors exercise only general supervision. It was found that the low-producing supervisors:

- check on employees more frequently
- give more detailed and frequent instructions
- limit employee's freedom to do job in own way

Workers who felt less closely supervised reported that they were better satisfied with their jobs and the company. We should note that the manner or attitude of the supervisor has an important bearing on whether employees perceive supervision as being close or general.

These findings are another way of saying that supervision does not mean standing over the employee and telling him what to do and when and how to do it. The more effective supervisor tells his employees what is required, giving general instructions.

COMMUNICATION

Supervisors of high-production units consider communication as one of the most important aspects of their job. Effective communication is used by these supervisors to achieve better interpersonal relations and improved employee motivation. Low-production supervisors do not rate communications as highly important.

High-producing supervisors find that an important aid to more effective communication is listening. They are ready to listen to both personal problems or interests and questions about the work. This does not mean that they are *nosey* or meddle in their employees' personal lives, but rather that they show a willingness to listen, and do listen, if their employees wish to discuss problems.

These supervisors inform employees about forthcoming changes in work; they discuss agency policy with employees; and they make sure that each employee knows how well he is doing. What these supervisors do is use two-way communication effectively. Unless the supervisor freely imparts information, he will not receive information in return.

Attitudes and perception are frequently affected by communication or the lack of it. Research surveys reveal that many supervisors are not aware of their employees' attitudes, nor do they know what personal reactions their supervision arouses. Through frank discussion with employees, they have been surprised to discover employee beliefs about which they were ignorant. Discussion sometimes reveals that the supervisor and his employees have totally different impressions about the same event. The supervisor should be constantly on the alert for misconceptions about his words and deeds. He must remember that, although his actions are perfectly clear to himself, they may be, and frequently are, viewed differently by employees.

Failure to communicate information results in misconceptions and false assumptions. What you say and how you say it will strongly affect your employees' attitudes and perceptions. By giving them available information, you can prevent misconceptions; by discussion, you may be able to change attitudes; by questioning, you can discover what the perceptions and assumptions really are. And it need hardly be added that actions should conform very closely to words.

If we were to attempt to reduce the above discussion on communication to rules, we would have a long list which would be based on one cardinal principle: Don't make assumptions!

- Don't assume that your employees know; tell them.
- Don't assume that you know how they feel; find out.
- Don't assume that they understand; clarify.

20 SUPERVISORY HINTS

1. Avoid inconsistency.
2. Always give employees a chance to explain their action before taking disciplinary action. Don't allow too much time for a "cooling off" period before disciplining an employee.
3. Be specific in your criticisms.
4. Delegate responsibility wisely.
5. Do not argue or lose your temper, and avoid being impatient.
6. Promote mutual respect and be fair, impartial, and open-minded.
7. Keep in mind that asking for employees' advice and input can be helpful in decision making.
8. If you make promises, keep them.
9. Always keep the feelings, abilities, dignity and motives of your staff in mind.
10. Remain loyal to your employees' interests.
11. Never criticize employees in front of others, or treat employees like children.
12. Admit mistakes. Don't place blame on your employees, or make excuses.
13. Be reasonable in your expectations, give complete instructions, and establish well-planned goals.
14. Be knowledgeable about office details and procedures, but avoid becoming bogged down in details.
15. Avoid supervising too closely or too loosely. Employees should also view you as an approachable supervisor.
16. Remember that employees' personal problems may affect job performance, but become involved only when appropriate.
17. Work to develop workers, and to instill a feeling of cooperation while working toward mutual goals.
18. Do not overpraise or underpraise, be properly appreciative.
19. Never ask an employee to discipline someone for you.
20. A complaint, even if unjustified, should be taken seriously.

NOTES

www.ingramcontent.com/pod-product-compliance
Lightning Source LLC
Chambersburg PA
CBHW081815300426
44116CB00014B/2372